The Persian Gulf War: Saddam's Failed Invasion

The Persian Gulf War: Saddam's Failed Invasion

Titles in the History's Great Defeats series include:

The Aztecs: End of a Civilization
The British Empire: The End of Colonialism
The Cold War: Collapse of Communism
The Crusades: Failed Holy Wars
The French Revolution: The Fall of the Monarchy
The Indian Wars: From Frontier to Reservation
The Napoleonic Wars: Defeat of the Grand Army
The Third Reich: Demise of the Nazi Dream

HISTORY'S GREAT DEFEATS

The Persian Gulf War: Saddam's Failed Invasion

by Michael J. Martin

LUCENT
BOOKS®

THOMSON
————————— TM
GALE

San Diego • Detroit • New York • San Francisco • Cleveland
New Haven, Conn. • Waterville, Maine • London • Munich

THOMSON
＊ ™
GALE

LIBRARY OF CONGRESS CATALOGING-IN-PUBLICATION DATA

Martin, Michael J., 1948–
The Persian Gulf war: Saddam's failed invasion / by Michael J. Martin.
    p. cm. — (History's great defeats series)
Includes bibliographical references and index.
ISBN 1-59018-428-9 (hardback : alk. paper)
1. Persian Gulf War, 1991—Juvenile literature. I. Title. II. Series.
DS79.723.M37 2004
956.7044'2—dc22
                                                                            2004010560

Printed in the United States of America

Table of Contents

Foreword

H ISTORY IS FILLED with tales of dramatic encounters that sealed the fates of empires or civilizations, changing them or causing them to disappear forever. One of the best known events began in 334 B.C., when Alexander, king of Macedonia, led his small but formidable Greek army into Asia. In the short span of only ten years, he brought Persia, the largest empire the world had yet seen, to its knees, earning him the nickname forever after associated with his name— "the Great." The demise of Persia, which at its height stretched from the shores of the Mediterranean Sea in the west to the borders of India in the east, was one of history's most stunning defeats. It occurred primarily because of some fatal flaws in the Persian military system, disadvantages the Greeks had exploited before, though never as spectacularly as they did under Alexander.

First, though the Persians had managed to conquer many peoples and bring huge territories under their control, they had failed to create an individual fighting man who could compare with the Greek hoplite. A heavily armored infantry soldier, the hoplite fought in a highly effective and lethal battlefield formation—the phalanx. Possessed of better armor, weapons, and training than the Persians, Alexander's soldiers repeatedly crushed their Persian opponents. Second, the Persians for the most part lacked generals of the caliber of their Greek counterparts. And when Alexander invaded, Persia had the added and decisive disadvantage of facing one of the greatest generals of all time. When the Persians were defeated, their great empire was lost forever.

Other world powers and civilizations have fallen in a like manner. They have succumbed to some combination of inherent fatal flaws or disadvantages, to political and/or military mistakes, and even to the personal failings of their leaders.

Another of history's great defeats was the sad demise of the North American Indian tribes at the hands of encroaching European civilization from the sixteenth to nineteenth centuries. In this case, all of the tribes suffered from the same crippling disadvantages. Among the worst, they lacked the great numbers, the unity, and the advanced industrial and military hardware possessed by the Europeans. Still another example, one closer to our own time, was the resounding defeat of Nazi Germany by the Allies in 1945, which brought World War II, the most disastrous conflict in history, to a close. Nazi Germany collapsed for many reasons. But one of the most telling was that its leader, Adolf Hitler, sorely underestimated the material resources and human resolve of the Allies, especially the United States. In the end, Germany was in a very real sense submerged by a massive and seemingly relentless tidal wave of Allied bombs, tanks, ships, and soldiers.

Seen in retrospect, a good many of the fatal flaws, drawbacks, and mistakes that caused these and other great defeats from the pages of history seem obvious. It is only natural to wonder why, in each case, the losers did not realize their limitations and/or errors sooner and attempt to avert disaster. But closer examination of the events, social and political trends, and leading personalities involved usually reveals that complex factors were at play. Arrogance, fear, ignorance, stubbornness, innocence, and other attitudes held by nations, peoples, and individuals often colored and shaped their reactions, goals, and strategies. And it is both fascinating and instructive to reconstruct how such attitudes, as well as the fatal flaws and mistakes themselves, contributed to the losers' ultimate demise.

Each volume in Lucent Books' *History's Great Defeats* series is designed to provide the reader with diverse learning tools for exploring the topic at hand. Each well-informed, clearly written text is supported and enlivened by substantial quotes by the actual people involved, as well as by later historians and other experts; and these primary and secondary sources are carefully documented. Each volume also supplies the reader with an extensive Works Consulted list, guiding him or her to further research on the topic. These and other research tools, including glossaries and time lines, afford the reader a thorough understanding of how and why one of history's most decisive defeats occurred and how these events shaped our world.

The Seizure of
Introduction Kuwait

A T 2 A.M. ON August 2, 1990, Iraqi troops, tanks, and trucks began moving across the southeastern border of Iraq. Saddam Hussein, Iraq's ruler, had just launched an invasion of Kuwait, Iraq's
tiny but wealthy neighbor. Saddam was confident that the one thousand
T-72 tanks, nine hundred armored vehicles, and 120,000 soldiers he had
sent across the border would make quick work of Kuwaiti defense forces.

Saddam Hussein was correct in his assessment of Iraq's military
superiority—Kuwait's roughly sixteen thousand troops were over-
whelmed in less than twelve hours. But this turned out to be the only
correct judgment he would make in the next seven months. A series of
miscalcuations, both before and after the invasion, resulted in a devastating defeat for Iraq in a war against a coalition of forty nations.

To be fair, the administration of President George H.W. Bush made
serious mistakes of its own—mistakes that contributed to Saddam's misperceptions. Investigations suggest that April Glaspie, the U.S. ambassador to Iraq, acting under instructions from Washington, may have given
Saddam the impression that the United States would not oppose his
aggression. As Congressman Stephen Solarz noted, "By declaring that
we had no obligation to come to the defense of Kuwait, and by taking
no position on Iraq's border dispute with Kuwait, administration spokes-
men clearly contributed to a perception on Saddam's part that we would
not resist his use of force in the Gulf."[1] Still, there were signs that Saddam should have heeded. In response to Saddam's threats, the United
States staged naval maneuvers in the Persian Gulf in July; he was not
impressed, since he knew the United States had no troops in the area.

A Tempting Target

Some of Kuwait's own actions could be seen as further encouraging Iraqi aggression. Even as the Iraqi buildup continued along the border, Kuwait's meager defense forces came down off high alert. One reason the Kuwaitis were so complacent was that they had given Saddam's government $10 billion in aid during the eight-year Iran-Iraq War that had ended two years earlier. They could not comprehend that a nation they had helped so recently would turn on them. Yet, as author Theodore Draper has noted, they seemed to have forgotten that theirs was a country "too rich to be left alone and too weak to defend itself."[2]

A half hour after the invasion began, Kuwait requested help from the United States. By then, it was far too late. Outnumbered twenty six to one, the Kuwaiti defense forces were no match for the battle-hardened

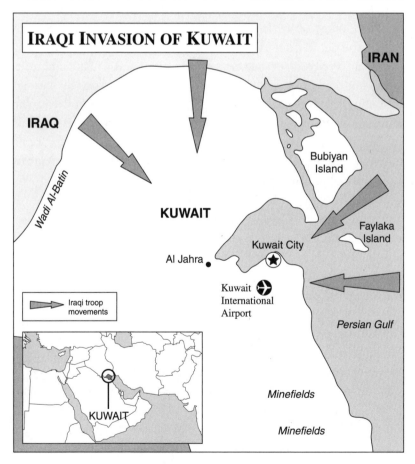

Iraqi troops. Within an hour, the Iraqis had reached the capital, Kuwait City. By 6 A.M. Iraqi tanks, jets, and artillery were attacking Dasman Palace, home of Kuwait's royal family, the Sabahs. Most of the royal family successfully made a frantic, high-speed escape in bulletproof limousines driven across the desert into neighboring Saudi Arabia.

Outnumbered and Outgunned

The royal family's escape was made possible by the heroic efforts of Kuwaiti defense forces at the palace. They were led by the popular Sheikh Fahd al-Ahmed al-Sabah, the half brother of the emir (Kuwait's ruler). Fahd gave his life to slow the Iraqi advance. An Iraqi soldier who later defected to Turkey gave this account: "He personally killed several soldiers around me and he inspired his men to keep up their defense. But they had no chance—we were too many. When the Sheik was shot, many of the Iraqis cheered. An officer ordered the Sheik's body to be put in front of a tank and run over."[3]

Brutality of this sort had always been a hallmark of Saddam's rule. Few who were familiar with his rule in Iraq were surprised by the tales of looting, torture, and execution that began filtering out of occupied Kuwait in the weeks to follow. "They took my best friend, Bedar, and the next day they dropped his body in the street," a Kuwaiti doctor told the *New York Times*. "They had wrapped his head in a Kuwaiti flag and fired three bullets into his skull."[4]

It appeared that the Iraqi behavior was intended to encourage Kuwaitis to leave. "They wanted them out . . . part of the massive looting and burning was designed to ensure that these people would have absolutely nothing to come home to,"[5] said one Bush administration official. By mid-September about two hundred thousand Kuwaiti citizens had fled the country.

Saddam's Claim

For his part, Saddam tried to promote the notion that Iraq had come to the aid of democratic forces within Kuwait. Tariq Aziz, Iraq's foreign minister, was instructed to say that Iraq had sent in troops in response to an appeal by "young revolutionaries."[6] In a meeting with U.S. officials in Baghdad after the invasion, Saddam insisted that the Iraqis were there only to show support for these nonexistent revolutionaries.

An Unimpressive First Impression

Major Martin Stanton was a U.S. military adviser in Saudi Arabia. He happened to be in Kuwait City on vacation when Iraqi forces invaded. Until the Iraqis took him captive, he reported on the situation from his hotel room using a cell phone. His impression of the Iraqi heavy armored divisions was not favorable and gave the first hints that the Iraqi army might not be as formidable as feared, as he indicated in his book *Road to Baghdad:*

> Two things surprised me about the armored column. First, three tanks were being towed by other tanks with tow bars. In the U.S. Army, broken vehicles such as those would be left for unit recovery teams in special armored recovery vehicles. . . . Here it seemed that if a vehicle was a mechanical failure, they just pulled it along. I noticed that each tank carried a set of tow bars. It made me wonder about their support echelons. The second thing I noticed was that each tank had crates of fruit and other food on top of the turret and back deck, and the crewmen appeared to be stuffing their faces as fast as they could. Obviously, they had stopped to loot a supermarket and were now chowing down their stolen goods. They seemed oblivious to the fact that in these urban surroundings, only a few Kuwaitis with rifles and RPGs [rocket-propelled grenades] could inflict tremendous damage upon them. The tanks chugged unmolested past the hotel and out of sight, however. A few of them had loose track flopping and folding under the drive sprocket, another sign of poor maintenance.

Iraqi officials claimed at first that their occupation of Kuwait would be brief. "We will withdraw when the situation becames stable and when Kuwait's free provisional government asks us to do so. This may not exceed a few days or a few weeks," claimed Saddam's Revolutionary Command Council. The council also hinted at the fate that would befall anyone who opposed the invasion: "We will make of the glorious Iraq and the dear Kuwait a graveyard for those who may be tempted to launch aggression and who are moved by the desire to invade and betray."[7]

In spite of these lofty words, virtually the entire world—even Arab leaders, who normally might refrain from criticizing a fellow Arab—concluded that it was Iraq that had been moved by a desire to invade and betray. The almost universally negative response was not at all what Saddam had been expecting. Yet those who best knew the Iraqi leader knew well that he was capable of such miscalculations.

Dreaming
Chapter 1   of Nebuchadnezzar

S ADDAM HUSSEIN HAD long been known to possess personality
traits that included brutality, stubborness, distrust of others, and,
above all, ambition. These traits had served him well in his drive
to seize—and then hold—power in Iraq. Yet these same traits helped
blind him to the likely consequences of invading Kuwait. In addition,
his strategy of eliminating potential challengers deprived him of the
talented leaders who might have helped him avert disaster.

Born in Tikrit in 1937, Saddam was raised mostly by a cruel uncle who had been an army officer. Saddam learned at an early age to
depend on himself. He also learned to use brute force. The other boys
in the village often mocked him because he had no father. He took to
carrying an iron bar to protect himself. Saddam hoped to become a
military officer, as his uncle was, but his grades were not good enough
for him to get into the Baghdad Military Academy, the institution
that supplied virtually all of Iraq's military officers.

Unable to get into the military, Saddam did what in his mind was
the next best thing. In 1957, at the age of twenty, he joined the Baath
Party, a revolutionary group that plotted to overthrow the dictator then
in power. Like Saddam, the Baathists believed in the use of force and intimidation to solve problems. In the years that followed, Saddam's ten-
dency toward violence became more pronounced—even as a teen he had
enjoyed going about with a pistol concealed inside his shirt. In 1958 he
was said to have killed a relative in a violent family argument. There is
some question whether the killing really happened or was simply a story
Saddam spread to convince others of his ruthlessness.

There is little doubt, however, that he was involved in a murder plot in 1959. This was the attempted assasination of Abd al-Karin Qassim, Iraq's leader at the time. The plot was unsuccessful. Shot in the leg during the attack, Saddam was fortunate to escape to Egypt. He would spend the next four years in Cairo—the only time in his life that Saddam spent more than a few days outside Iraq.

From Bully to Baath Party Leader

Saddam enrolled in the law school at Cairo University, but showed only limited interest in or aptitude for the law. Hussein Abdel Meguid, the owner of a restaurant where Saddam spent most of his days, recalls that Saddam rarely went to class. Moreover, his belligerence resulted

By 1970, when this photo was taken, Saddam Hussein had become one of the most powerful officials in Iraq's ruling Baath Party.

in frequent verbal and physical confrontations with the restaurant's other patrons. Many years later, Meguid expressed amazement that Saddam had become Iraq's leader. "I couldn't believe," he said, "that such a bully who was picking fights all the time could grow up to be president of Iraq."[8]

Saddam returned to Iraq in 1963. The next five years were a time of political instability that saw both Saddam's fortunes and those of the Baath Party rise and fall. Eventually, in 1968, the Baath Party managed to establish a stable regime. By 1969 Saddam had been named deputy chairman of the Revolutionary Command Council, the second most powerful position in the party. Soon after, he reorganized the secret police, putting them under his control and giving himself free rein to terrorize or eliminate anyone who posed a threat to his own power. In his book *Desert Victory*, author Norman Friedman noted how the creation of fear was an integral part of Saddam's "work":

> The Iraqi Ba'athists depended on terror, apparently to a degree extraordinary even in the Third World, to maintain their position. In a manner reminiscent of [the late Soviet leader

Fear, Grandeur, and Flunkies

In their book *Saddam Hussein: A Political Biography,* Efraim Karsh and Inari Rautsi describe how the onetime poor boy from Tikrit quickly developed a taste for the kind of wealthy lifestyle that reflected his grand ambitions:

> Having established himself at the Presidential Palace, Saddam ran the country through a combination of deep fear and awesome grandeur, typical of Iraq's imperial rulers. Although his appetite for pomp was not to assume preposterous proportions until the last stages of the Iran-Iraq War, it was already visible in the first days of his Presidency. In contrast with the humble image he sought to project to his subjects, Saddam quickly got accustomed to the small privileges attending his new position. His wardrobe expanded to no fewer than 200 expensive suits, uniforms and tribal costumes for every occasion. A luxurious yacht was ordered from a Danish shipyard. One of Saddam's visitors gave a vivid description of the President's pomp: "he was dogged by an obsequious flunky carrying a large box. Every few minutes, Saddam, without turning round, would reach for a giant Havana, light up, take a few puffs, [and] stub it out, only to reach for another."

Joseph] Stalin, they used fabricated plots to justify mass executions and torture. They knew that they could only be ousted by coup, that is, only by conspiracy, and therefore their primary concern was to eliminate all possible internal threats.[9]

One of Saddam's instruments of terror was the Qasr al-Nihaya—the Palace of the End. This was a prison where enemies of the party were tortured. Saddam often conducted interrogations after victims were beaten and tortured. "He had the authority, with one word, to decide if you stayed alive or died,"[10] recalled a journalist who was questioned by Saddam in 1969.

Saddam's unchallengeable authority ensured that potential rivals would not live long enough to pose any real threat. Later on, this reputation for brutality and intolerance for opposing views ensured that, in his position as Iraqi's leader, few people would dare give him advice that might conflict with his own opinions. Consequently, when he decided to invade Kuwait, no one was willing to warn him of the dangers.

Terror from the Top

For most of the 1970s, Saddam was content to remain second in command while ruling from behind the scenes. He could safely continue consolidating power because Iraq's president at the time was his older cousin Ahmad Hasan al-Bakr. As the decade drew to a close, al-Bakr was becoming old and weak. In July 1979 Saddam took over the presidency.

Saddam wasted no time in establishing the tone of his rule. In the weeks after he assumed power, Saddam had twenty-one members of his own cabinet executed—including one of his closest friends. As many as five hundred senior members of the Revolutionary Command Council were also done away with. "He who is closest to me is farthest from me when he does wrong,"[11] explained Saddam.

Outsiders who met Iraq's leader were under no illusions as to the sort of man they were dealing with. "He is an extremely shrewd, cold-blooded, clever thug," said a British diplomat who had face-to-face dealings with Saddam. "Human life means nothing to him."[12] Dan Goodgame, a correspondent for *Time* magazine, recalled the chill he felt during his first encounter with Saddam: "On meeting him, a visitor is first struck by his eyes, crackling with alertness and at the same time cold and remorseless as snake eyes on the sides of dice. They are the eyes of a killer."[13]

The Man Who Would Be King

But besides being a killer, Saddam was a man of towering ambition. He saw himself as an invincible warrior and empire builder, a man destined to return the Arab world to past glories. He was well aware that one of the Arab world's greatest heroes, Saladin, had also been born in Tikrit. Saladin was a twelfth-century Muslim commander who successfully fought against the Christians during the Crusades. He captured Jerusalem, made himself ruler of Egypt and Syria, and controlled a swath of territory stretching from North Africa to what is now northern Iraq.

Saddam made no secret of his view of himself as a new Saladin. In a speech he made just two weeks before his forces invaded Kuwait, Saddam claimed that the situation in the Middle East was similar to that during the Crusades and hinted at the regional support he believed would soon be forthcoming. "But the Crusades," he added, "also remind us of that well-known historic fact that victory in the end was for the Arabs as a result of joint action."[14] Three months after the invasion, in an interview with a Japanese television reporter, Saddam described the coming war with the forces allied against Iraq as "a second Crusade."[15]

But the leader who most inspired Saddam seems to have been Nebuchadnezzar, the king of ancient Babylon. Nebuchadnezzar was a master builder and his Hanging Gardens of Babylon were one of the Seven Wonders of the Ancient World. In 587 B.C. Nebuchadnezzar put down a Jewish revolt in Judah, at the time a captive state of Babylon. He destroyed Jerusalem and brought thousands of Jews back to Babylon in captivity. Saddam repeated this story often and did not hide the fact that he hoped to follow in the footsteps of the great Babylonian king. He even began a giant project to reconstruct ancient Babylon. Millions of bricks were baked, many inscribed with the words: "The Babylon of Nebuchadnezzar was reconstructed in the era of Saddam Hussein."[16]

For Saddam, war offered a return to past glories. Qadisiyah was a famous battle fought between Arabs and Persians in A.D. 636. Although outnumbered six to one, the Arabs triumphed. In 1980, when Saddam began his war with Iran—the modern-day Persia—he called it "the second Qadisiyah." An early indication of the grandiose plans Saddam had in mind for his people—and himself—was an odd two-page statement

Saddam meets with Iraqi president Ahmad Hasan al-Bakr in 1978. The following year, Saddam assumed the presidency.

that ran in the London *Times* only a year after he assumed power. An official release of the Iraqi government, it could not have run without Saddam's approval:

Iraq was more than once the springboard for a new civilization in the Middle East and the question is now pertinently asked, with a leader like this man, the wealth of oil resources and a forceful people like the Iraqis, will she repeat her former glories and the name of Saddam Hussein link up with that of Hammurabi, Ashurbanipal, al-Mansur and Harun al-Rashid? To be sure, they have not really achieved half of what he has

"Like a Black Hole . . . "

Meeting Saddam Hussein could be an intimidating experience—even for people who did not have to fear being killed by him. Canadian writer and film producer Paul Roberts met Saddam for an interview in the presidential palace in 1990. He recalled the chilling incident in his book *The Demonic Comedy:*

> When he looked up it was directly into my eyes, clearly calculated to be that way too, but the shock hit like a column of iced mercury pumped up the spine. He didn't blink either. He didn't stand, and when I reached out my hand, paused a beat before extending a limp, dry, cool, dead appendage. It could have been rubber.

> I looked back at the eyes and realized what was most unnerving about them was there was nobody behind them. Not the emptiness of peace you see in the yogi or rimpoche's eyes, this was the total absence of something most people possess in varying degrees on varying days. Life? No, it was much more than the deadness of the palace beyond. It was a missing part and a part as crucial as head or limbs—probably the part we used to call the "soul."

> It was not a pleasant experience, because you can't *not* have a soul. Like a black hole, his soul must have imploded under the weight of its own darkness and, though there, was invisible, gave out nothing, and viewed all in terms of mere utility.

> I was of no use to him, it was clear.

already done at the helm of the Ba'th Arab Socialist Party, [and] he is still only 44.[17]

A Deadly Exercise in Futility

About the same time the *Times* piece ran, Saddam began his war with Iran—a war that would cost billions of dollars and cripple Iraq's economic development. As he would a decade later in Kuwait, Saddam insisted on directing the war himself, despite the fact that he had no military training. He was not a particularly able commander. After some successes in the first months, the army became bogged down. Still, Saddam received a great deal of military support from the United States by selling himself as a ruler who would restrain the anti-Americanism of the Islamic fundamentalists who had recently come to power in Iran.

When the war ended after eight years of fighting, the situation on the ground was virtually unchanged—despite the fact that an estimated 375,000 Iraqi men had been killed or maimed. Casualties were never a concern of Saddam's. According to one famous story, a senior general once warned Saddam that an attack he had ordered would lead to heavy loss of life. Saddam invited the general into the next room to discuss the matter—and then shot him dead.

Ever distrustful of the military, Saddam used the same strategy he had once employed in his rise to political power: literally eliminating potential rivals. His goal was to ensure that his huge army never turned on him. Judith Miller and Laurie Mylroie outlined his strategy in their book *Saddam Hussein and the Crisis in the Gulf*:

> He sought first to hollow out the institutions of the military, to ensure that only party stalwarts would survive to form a new and trustworthy officer corps. . . . Political loyalty became the primary criterion for officers' promotion. But Saddam can

Slain Iraqi soldiers, victims of the Iran-Iraq War, lie on the battlefield. The eight-year conflict resulted in an estimated 375,000 Iraqi casualties.

never be sure that he has the army's loyalty or respect. His hold over the army has always been a problem. He has no military experience and no base in the army. Thus, Saddam has been careful not to let any individual military leader become too powerful. Officers are frequently rotated and those that might become dangerous are executed.[18]

Ironically, Saddam's distrust of his own officers virtually guaranteed that his grand dreams of empire would not come to fruition in Iran or Kuwait. In effect, Saddam's policies deprived him of his ablest military commanders.

Saddam's Motivation

Iraq emerged from war with Iran financially ruined, but with a million-man army that made it the leading military power in the Persian Gulf. But all those idle soldiers presented Saddam with real problems. With the economy in such bad shape, people were becoming discontented. Food was in such short supply that many Iraqis had to resort to buying from black marketers at high prices. Saddam knew that some Iraqis were blaming him for the situation. If something were not done soon, he risked being overthrown by ambitious or disgruntled military commanders.

Saddam's sense of desperation was heightened by the $80 billion he had borrowed to pay for the war and to protect ordinary Iraqis from the kind of hardships that might turn them against it—and him. By 1990 the bills were coming due. Although Iraq had plenty of oil reserves, they could not be sold at a high enough price to pay back the debt. Oil prices were falling because nations such as Kuwait and the United Arab Emirates were increasing their own production. In Saddam's eyes, these countries might as well have declared war on Iraq.

"For every single dollar drop in the price of a barrel of oil, our loss amounts to $1 billion a year," he told a gathering of Arab leaders in Baghdad in May 1990. "War," he added, "is fought with soldiers and much harm is done by explosions, killing, and coup attempts—but it is also done by economic means . . . this is in fact a kind of war against Iraq."[19] He hinted that Iraq would have to take bold action if something were not done soon.

Iraqi soldiers in combat during the Iran-Iraq War. Iraq emerged from the conflict as the leading military power in the Persian Gulf.

Saddam had always been a man who preferred direct action. Sahib al-Hakim, an Iraqi who lost twenty-two family members to Saddam's executioners, recalled a story told to him by the former governor of Najaf province. It illustrates how, when it came to solving problems, Saddam's favored method was the use of force:

> There was a time in the 1970s when the governor needed money for some projects in Najaf. So he went to see Saddam. They sat on opposite ends of a long table. He asked for help. When he was finished, Saddam asked him, "You need money?" He answered, "Yes, I need money." So Saddam motioned to his bodygard and asked for the bodyguard's gun. He shoved the gun to the other end of the table and said, "Take it. And solve your problems yourself."[20]

The Kuwait Solution

In Saddam's mind, then, invading Kuwait was a rational act that had numerous advantages. Meanwhile, his ambition and his fear of being overthrown blinded him to the risks involved. He saw the invasion as another step in his quest to become the unquestioned leader of the Arab world. Making Kuwait part of Iraq fit perfectly with Saddam's oft-stated notions of Iraq's place in the Middle East:

> The glory of the Arabs stems from the glory of Iraq. Throughout history, whenever Iraq became mighty and flourished, so did the Arab nation. This is why we are striving to make Iraq mighty, formidable and developed.[21]

Just as important, swallowing up Kuwait would erase much of Saddam's debt problem. Iraq owed Kuwait at least $17 billion (Saddam's attack on Kuwait has been compared to robbing the bank to which one owes money). Jeffrey Record, author of *Hollow Victory*, quotes former assistant secretary of state Richard Murphy on Iraq's debt problem: "Saddam came to realize that he was being regarded as one of the world's worst credit risks and was facing bankruptcy," and he reasoned, not illogically, that "to get out of bankruptcy, you rob a bank."[22] In addition, control of rich Kuwaiti oil fields would add greatly to Iraq's oil revenues. But the effects would go far beyond increased oil production. Kuwait's oil fields would give Iraq control of an additional 15 percent of the world's oil wealth, endowing Saddam with the clout to set world oil prices to his liking.

Saddam had long claimed that Kuwait rightfully belonged to Iraq. Not long after the tiny country obtained its independence from Britain in 1961, Iraq had unsuccessfully tried to conquer it. Now, by "returning" Kuwait to Iraq, Saddam could sell himself to fellow Iraqis as a conquering hero, and Kuwait's riches could be used to finance ambitious economic programs that would keep ordinary Iraqis content—and ensure that Saddam remained safely in power. Furthermore, by threatening and intimidating nations outside of Iraq, Saddam added to his authority at home by appearing to be too strong for anyone to stand up against.

Revenge also figured into Saddam's calculations. He felt that his war with Iran had protected nations such as Kuwait and Saudi Arabia from Islamic fundamentalists. Yet these countries were not appropriately grateful for the sacrifices Iraq had made on their behalf. Saddam was particularly angry with Kuwait, a nation he considered a parasite. He demanded that its leaders forgive most of the debt Iraq owed the government. Their refusal to do so convinced him they were

---

A Don with a Difference

In their book *Saddam Hussein and the Crisis in the Gulf,* Judith Miller and Laurie Mylroie discussed Saddam's favorite movie:

> Saddam Hussein loves *The Godfather.* It is his favorite movie, one he has seen many times. He is especially fascinated by Don Corleone, a poor boy made good, whose respect for family is exceeded only by his passion for power. The iron-willed character of the Don may perhaps be the most telling model for the enigmatic figure that rules Iraq. Both come from dirt-poor peasant villages; both sustain their authority by violence; and for both, family is key, the key to power. Family is everything, or "almost" everything, because Saddam, like the Godfather, ultimately trusts no one, not even his next of kin. For both, calculation and discipline, loyalty and ruthlessness are the measure of a man's character.

> There is, however, a difference. Where the Don was a private man, obsessed with secrecy, seeking always to conceal his crimes behind a veil of anonymity, Saddam is a public figure who usurped political power and seizes every opportunity to advertise his might in order to impress upon his countrymen that there is no alternative to his rule. To visit Iraq is to enter the land of Big Brother.

---

not giving him the respect he deserved. In a last-ditch effort to forestall Iraqi military action, Egyptian president Hosni Mubarak asked Saddam to meet with the emir of Kuwait at a conference in Jiddah, Saudi Arabia. Saddam agreed to meet with the emir, Sheikh Jaber al-Ahmed al-Sabah, on August 1, 1990, to discuss their differences, but at the last minute the emir decided not to attend. Saddam saw the emir's withdrawal as a supreme insult.

The slight to Iraq's honor was now to be avenged. As a bonus, Saddam thought, his revenge would also ensure his political survival, with very little risk to himself or his nation. None of his advisers dared tell him otherwise.

Saddam Against

Chapter 2 # the World

ALTHOUGH THE INVASION of Kuwait went according to plan, Saddam's ignorance of the way other nations viewed him led to numerous political miscalculations. Those blunders quickly isolated Iraq from its neighbors—and from virtually the entire world—and helped lead to his eventual military defeat.

The first mistake Saddam made was to assume that the other Persian Gulf countries would not oppose Iraq swallowing up Kuwait. At first glance this assumption seems justified, since the wealthy Kuwaitis were envied more than they were liked. Still, Saddam never expected that other Persian Gulf nations would be pleased with his actions. In fact, political observers believe that intimidation was likely one of his goals. He did not believe, however, that other Arab countries would do much more than grumble. Their decision to take up arms against Iraq seems to have caught him by surprise.

Egypt, the oldest and most populous country in the Middle East, had long considered itself the leader of the Arab world. Its people, therefore, did not share Saddam's belief that he was a modern-day Saladin or Nebuchadnezzar. Moreover, standing by while Iraq gobbled up other sovereign nations seemed unwise—especially since there was no guarantee that Kuwait would be the last country Iraq would want to assimilate.

A Shocking Saudi Move

Saddam also did not expect another major Mideast power, Saudi Arabia, to join in the opposition to his move. Since Saudi Arabia contains Islam's holiest shrines, Saddam believed that its leaders would never dare allow non-Muslims to establish a presence there. This proved to be a grave miscalculation, one prompted largely by Iraqi aggression. On August 3, Iraqi troops advanced six miles into Saudi Arabia, a clear violation of the nonaggression pact the two nations had signed in 1989. The Iraqis assured the Saudis that the incursion had been a mistake and would not happen again. But after two more incursions, the Saudis concluded that an invasion was imminent. They felt they had no choice but to call on the United States for help.

Consequently, not only did Saudi Arabia supply its own troops to fight against Iraq, it allowed a half million U.S. troops to use its bases and ports, as well as train on its soil. In fact, the use of Saudi territory provided coalition forces with a huge advantage. Saudi Arabia had more than thirty modern air bases that could accommodate virtually any kind of aircraft, from combat fighters to huge cargo planes. In addition, the country had eight modern ports with facilities capable of handling most kinds of cargo. Furthermore, Saudi Arabia was rich in oil—a necessity for the machines used by modern armies. The abundance of Saudi oil meant that very little of the fuel for the war effort had to be shipped into the area beforehand. Without the help of Saudi Arabia, coalition forces could never have mounted a response to Saddam's aggression in such a short time. As one defense policy analyst put it, "Saddam Hussein could not have threatened a neighbor better suited to accommodate a rapid and massive foreign military buildup on his very doorstep."[23]

No Soviet Support

With few exceptions, countries around the world condemned Iraq's unprovoked aggression. Even the Soviet Union, a longtime ally of Iraq, dealt Saddam a nasty surprise. The Soviet economy was struggling badly and the nation's leaders decided they needed aid from Western countries more than they needed to maintain their relationship with Iraq. On August 6 the Soviet Union joined the UN Security Council in voting overwhelmingly to impose a worldwide embargo on trade with Iraq. The embargo eliminated about 90 percent of Iraq's imports and about 97 percent of its exports. Never before in its history had the United Nations adopted such sweeping sanctions. They became the most visible way to punish Iraq for its actions. With most countries refusing to buy Iraqi oil, Saddam's main source of income was cut off.

A U.S. Marine in Saudi Arabia fires a mortar shell as a training exercise. Saddam mistakenly believed that Saudi Arabia would refuse to host U.S. forces.

This, too, was something Saddam had failed to foresee. After all, he had gone into Kuwait to increase his income.

Meanwhile, British and U.S. naval forces set up a blockade to prevent ships from entering or leaving Iraq. It did not take long for the embargo to have an effect. It was said to cost the country $1.5 billion per month. Perhaps the most important function of the embargo was that it kept pressure on Iraq while land, sea, and air forces assembled in Saudi Arabia.

Saddam's biggest miscalculation, however, was thinking that the United States would be content to stand by while Iraq seized control of such a large portion of the world's oil reserves. Access to oil is absolutely crucial for Western economies, and no nation would be allowed to monopolize that access—a fact Saddam never seemed to fully grasp.

A Weakened Giant?

As with his other miscalculations, Saddam had at least some ground for believing that the United States would accede to his aggression. In

He Saw a Paper Tiger

In *The Saddam Hussein Reader,* a collection of essays on Iraq edited by Turi Munthe, Amatzia Baram writes about what he considered to be the Iraqi leader's biggest mistake:

> Saddam's greatest miscalculation, then, was his failure to predict the U.S. response to an Iraqi occupation of Kuwait. Taking at face value the popular post-Vietnam perception in the Third World of America as a paper tiger, Saddam did not believe that it had the stamina to fight a costly war against him. Whether this perception was right, he was certainly wrong in his assumption that any war against him would be costly for the Americans. . . .
>
> Even on January 15 Saddam still could not believe the United States would fight. The ambiguous positions of France and the Soviet Union, antiwar demonstrations in the West, and a pilgrimage of ex–world leaders to Baghdad helped convince him that there was no need to hurry. Surrounded by yes men, Saddam wrongly believed that, in the ground campaign, his soldiers would still fight to the death and inflict enough casualties on the coalition to deadlock the war. This belief, too, was in error.

particular, he recalled that the United States had proven unwilling to keep taking casualties during the Vietnam War. He believed, therefore, that Americans would never support another bloody war. Back in July he had boasted to April Glaspie, the U.S. ambassador to Iraq, that his country had been hardened by the Iran-Iraq War in a way that the United States could never understand. "American society is unable to sustain 10,000 fatalities in one battle,"[24] he explained to her.

Therefore, when President Bush announced on August 8 that U.S. troops were on their way to Saudi Arabia, Saddam was not overly concerned. Instead, he expressed pleasure that Kuwait was now part of Iraq: "Thank God, we are now one people, one state that will be the pride of the Arabs."[25]

Saudi Arabia at Risk

Meanwhile, members of the U.S. intelligence community were gravely concerned about Saudi Arabia's fate. Saddam had used tens of thousands more troops than he actually needed to capture Kuwait. It seemed quite possible that he was intent on rolling southward into the Saudi oil fields as well. The desert in that part of the Middle East was perfectly suited for the movement of large armored forces. If Saddam decided to move into Saudi Arabia there was little anyone could do to stop him.

The operation to protect Saudi Arabia was given the name Operation Desert Shield. In the beginning, Desert Shield was, indeed, strictly defensive. Bush, however, hinted that the United States was prepared to do more than act as a shield. "This will not stand," he promised, "this aggression against Kuwait."[26]

Total Misunderstanding

Saddam did not take such statements seriously. He failed to understand that the invasion of Kuwait had completely changed the relationship between Iraq and the United States. At a meeting with U.S. diplomat Joseph C. Wilson IV, he warned that the United States would be defeated if it attacked Iraq, then suggested that Iraq might make a much better ally than Saudi Arabia for the United States. Perhaps the best example of how ignorant Saddam was of the U.S.

U.S. troops march across the Saudi desert toward the Iraqi border in 1991. Saddam greatly underestimated the scope of the U.S. response to the invasion of Kuwait.

In 1990 Saddam poses with Europeans he had taken hostage. The Iraqi leader intended to use the hostages as human shields against the possibility of U.S. bombings.

reaction was the manner in which he prefaced a comment about Sheikh Jaber al-Ahmed al-Sabah, the emir of Kuwait, during his meeting with Wilson: "By the way, say hello to President Bush. And tell him that Jaber and his clique are finished; they're history. The Sabah family are has-beens."[27]

In the meantime, still underestimating the shock his aggression had caused other Arab countries, Saddam worked to unravel the coalition of forces that had lined up against him. He tried to portray himself as a hero to the millions of Arabs who resented the influence of Israel and the West. Hoping to win the favor of such people, Saddam offered to withdraw from Kuwait if Israel would also withdraw from the territories it had acquired during the 1967 and 1973 wars. Saddam knew there was little chance of an Israeli withdrawal, but such statements made for good publicity. For good measure, he also promised to attack Israel if Kuwait were attacked.

Saddam's Strategies

Indeed, Saddam's threats against Israel resonated with some Palestinians. But since he had previously paid little attention to the Palestinian cause, most Arab leaders continued to distrust him. They did so even after he encouraged them to rise up against Westerners he described as "infidel invaders . . . drunken, pork-eating whoremongers infected with AIDS."[28]

Other moves by Saddam also backfired because of his flawed perceptions. For example, in August he ordered all Westerners living in Kuwait to report to three hotels. From there, hundreds of British, French, American, Australian, Dutch, Italian, and Japanese nationals were taken for what he called "relocation" to Iraq. Saddam called these people "foreign guests," but they were, in fact, hostages. Once in Iraq some of these so-called guests were held against their will at strategic military and industrial sites. Saddam was using them as human shields against the possibility of U.S. bombing. Saddam tried to sell the hostage taking as an act of peace. At one point he appeared on television trying to comfort an obviously frightened British child being held as hostage. The incident was so bizarre that it outraged the rest of the world and hardened resolve to do something about him.

Day after day, the coalition's buildup continued. Still, Saddam discounted the possibility that those forces would eventually move to eject him from Kuwait. Once again, this was a fundamental misperception on Saddam's part. As defense analyst Norman Friedman explained, "He seems to have considered the buildup largely a gesture to placate the Saudis rather than the beginning of an assault force."[29]

Upping the Ante

To be sure, in the beginning the United States claimed that the forces assembling in the Saudi desert were strictly for defense. However, Bush's announcement on November 8 should have made U.S. intentions crystal clear. There were two hundred thousand troops in Saudi Arabia at that point. Bush announced that he was going to double that number in order to provide, as he said, "an adequate offensive military option."[30]

Saddam overlooked the fact that Bush's order created a momentum for war that could be halted only by an Iraqi withdrawal from Kuwait.

There was, after all, no way that almost a half million troops could be kept in the region indefinitely. At the urging of the United States, the United Nations passed a Security Council resolution on November 29 that set a January 15, 1991, deadline for Iraqi forces to leave Kuwait. That firm deadline and the huge number of additional troops arriving in the region, plus the blow to U.S. prestige if it were to let the deadline pass without action, should, experts contend, have convinced Saddam that he had no choice but to leave Kuwait.

It did not. On the day the UN resolution passed, Saddam spoke to a youth group in Baghdad. He boasted that Iraq was prepared for war and was "neither shaken nor panicked by the air and sea fleets of America and its aides."[31] Defending the seizure of Kuwait as a peaceful enterprise that would benefit all Arabs, he spoke of the greatness of Iraq. Then he warned the United States about the dangers of a confrontation. He ended with advice for Bush—advice that, as some commentators have noted, he would have been well advised to follow himself before deciding to invade Kuwait. "He who seeks war," Saddam thundered, "will by himself bear the responsibility for its consequences before God and his people."[32]

Outdated Defenses

Even as he refused to believe that war was imminent, Saddam prepared for some level of conflict, wherever it might come. Yet he based the defense of Kuwait on Iraq's experience in its eight-year conflict with Iran; that is, he worked from the assumption that retaliation would come in the form of infantry attack. However, he failed to take into account that the Iran-Iraq War, with its trench warfare and high casualty rate, was more like World War I than any modern war. Saddam did not seem to realize that his adversaries had long ago designed ways to go over, around, and through such defenses.

What Saddam's combat engineers tried to devise was a modern-day Verdun, the World War I battlefield where more than a million men were killed or wounded. They erected huge sand barriers, built miles of tank traps, dug trenches, and planted minefields and strung barbed wire. Many of the trenches were filled with oil that could be set ablaze at a moment's notice. Behind these obstacles were tanks, mortars, and artillery. Saddam seemed to believe that attacking such a defensive network would be so costly for coalition forces that they would end up settling for his occupation of Kuwait.

Drifting Toward War

Instead of dealing with the sobering reality of the January 15 deadline for withdrawal, Saddam traded threats and warnings with the West. On a New Year's Eve visit to his troops in Kuwait, Saddam made it clear that he was not intimidated by the massive buildup across the Saudi border. Speaking in heroic terms, he claimed that it was the coalition that was showing signs of weakness:

> Let them mass whatever numbers they can, because God will protect us from evil and save Iraq. To Bush's disappointment, the unprecedented U.S.-dominated buildup has failed to force Iraq to blink. At a time when the U.S. waits impatiently for a sign indicating Iraqi readiness to compromise, Iraq is growing more and more resolved not to cede any of its rights.[33]

On January 9 a last-ditch attempt to negotiate a peace was made in Geneva, Switzerland. Secretary of State James Baker represented the United States and Foreign Minister Tariq Aziz represented Iraq.

A Momentous Decision

James H. Webb Jr., a former secretary of the navy, was one of the many seasoned observers who realized how critical President Bush's decision to double U.S. troop deployments to Saudi Arabia was. Jeffrey Record quotes Webb in his book *Hollow Victory:*

> [By] sending such a huge commitment of American ground forces, and at the same time escalating the rhetoric of the confrontation, the President has placed himself—and our troops—in a doubly unfortunate situation. First, the so-called logic of war and the danger of our country losing its credibility makes it difficult to reduce or adjust these ground forces, since we might be perceived as "backing down" without having forced the Iraqi army out of Kuwait. Second, since a majority of the U.S. Army is now overseas, and since two-thirds of the operational forces of our Marine Corps will soon be sitting in the desert, we cannot maintain the size of our commitment for much longer without running into problems of human endurance. . . .

> In other words, the size and structure of our military commitment, rather than external events, risk becoming the dominant factors in whether force should be used.

No Criticism Allowed

In testimony before the House Armed Services Committee before Desert Storm began, a political psychologist employed by the CIA gave his impressions of Saddam Hussein. His assessment is quoted in Jeffrey Record's *Hollow Victory:*

> While he is psychologically in touch with reality, he is often politically out of touch with reality. Saddam's worldview is narrow and distorted, and he has scant experience out of the Arab world. . . . He is surrounded by sycophants, who are cowed by Saddam's well-founded reputation for brutality and are afraid to contradict him. He has ruthlessly eliminated perceived threats to his power and equates criticism with disloyalty. While Hussein is not psychotic, he has a strong paranoid orientation. He is ready for retaliation and, not without reason, sees himself as surrounded by enemies. But he ignores his role in creating those enemies, and righteously threatens his targets.

A political psychologist with the CIA once profiled Saddam as a paranoiac who responded to perceived threats with terrific brutality.

It soon became apparent that Aziz had no freedom to negotiate. To keep an eye on him, Saddam's half brother Barzan sat on his right and Saddam's personal interpreter to his left. As a result, no progress was made at all toward a settlement. Aziz's comments echoed Saddam's wishful, unrealistic thinking: "Your alliance will crumble and you will be left lost in the desert," he told Baker. "You don't know the desert because you have never ridden on a horse or camel."[34]

Back in Iraq on the same day, Saddam vowed that Iraq would achieve a decisive victory if it came to war. "If the Americans are involved," he thundered, "you will see how we will make them swim in their [own] blood."[35]

Afterward, at a press conference, Baker tried to explain to the world—and to Saddam—the extent of the misjudgments the Iraqi leader had made:

> There have been too many Iraqi miscalculations. The Iraqi government miscalculated the international response to the invasion of Kuwait, expecting the world community to stand idly by while Iraqi forces systematically pillaged a peaceful neighbor. It miscalculated the response, I think, to the barbaric policy of holding thousands of foreign hostages. . . . And it miscalculated that it could divide the international community and gain something thereby from its aggression. So let us hope that Iraq does not miscalculate again. . . . The path of peace remains open.[36]

Stubborn Beyond Belief

Despite Baker's expressions of hope, Saddam refused to budge. He continued to link any withdrawal from Kuwait with an Israeli withdrawal from its occupied territories. This was a precondition the West found unacceptable, since acceding to it would reward Iraq's aggression. Many people, including many in the Bush administration, found Saddam's misperceptions inexplicable. In their view the Iraqi leader was being willfully ignorant of the obvious.

Some observers have sought to explain Saddam's stubbornness in terms of the difference between the way conflicts are resolved in Arab culture and the way they are resolved in Western culture. According to Raphael Patai, author of *The Arab Mind*, "In every conflict, [Arabs] tend to feel that their honor is at stake and that to give in, even as little as an inch, would diminish their self-respect and dignity. Even to take the first step toward ending a conflict would be regarded as a sign of weakness which, in turn, would greatly damage one's honor."[37] According to this school of thought, Saddam's

U.S. secretary of state James Baker (right) greets Iraq's foreign minister Tariq Aziz at the 1991 Geneva conference. The peace-seeking mission was a failure.

notion of honor and dignity have made it impossible for him to back down over Kuwait.

While Saddam's behavior seemed self-defeating to most Western observers, it did have its benefits. In much of the Middle East, standing up to the United States was equivalent to standing up to the widely hated Israelis. Saddam's defiance helped promote his self-created image as a champion of the Arab world.

Saddam Could Not Quit Kuwait

In the end, argues defense analyst Jeffrey Record, Saddam, whose every action was calculated to ensure his own survival, had compelling reasons for staying in Kuwait. Chief among them was that "leaving without a fight was more politically dangerous to Saddam than fighting and losing. An honorable military defeat was preferable to a humiliating political capitulation without firing a shot."[38] In other words, Saddam's hold on Iraq was based on an image of absolute and overwhelming power. He may well have feared that fellow Iraqis would see withdrawal from Kuwait as a sign of weakness and rise up against him.

Washington Post columnist Charles Krauthammer made the same point in a slightly different way. For Saddam, he wrote, capitulation "meant humiliation and—quite possibly—as often follows in the Arab world—death."[39] If Record's and Krauthammer's suspicions were accurate, Saddam's biggest mistake was putting himself in a position from which he simply could not back down.

"Colleague of the Devil"

For whatever reason, the January 15 deadline passed without the slightest indication that Iraq was planning on leaving Kuwait. Hours before the deadline, Saddam composed a letter to Bush showing that diplomacy was not one of his strengths. In the letter he addressed the president as "enemy of God and colleague of the devil":

> The glorious Iraqi people and I have listened thoroughly to your hysterical statements threatening terrible consequences for Iraq and threatening aggression and destruction if Iraq fails to comply with your terms of capitulation. Accursed be you and hopeless are your objectives.[40]

A Case of Poor Timing

In his book *Desert Victory,* Norman Friedman notes that Saddam picked a bad time to invade Kuwait:

> Unfortunately for Saddam Hussein, he invaded Kuwait at just the moment when the decline of the cold war freed the United Nations to do the peacekeeping or policing job for which it had been created in 1945. The Soviets, who in earlier times would surely have vetoed the U.S.-sponsored resolutions, this time supported them. The Soviet Union badly needed Western cooperation in its reconstruction, and its strategy was a combination of military/political disengagement (to save money and to release needed resources) and attempts to gain Western economic support. The Soviets therefore badly wanted to show that they were responsible members of the community of nations. They could not be seen as brooking aggression, particularly aggression for which no obvious justification had been advanced. The Chinese, who might have vetoed the resolution on the grounds that they represented an assault on the Third World, were inclined to support the United States, at least partly because they were more interested in resuming U.S. economic ties than in fomenting world disorder.

Saddam went on to boast that Iraq was well prepared for battle, and he offered Bush one last chance to "withdraw your armies and those of your allies from the land that is sacred to Arabs and Muslims."[41] He also called for a fresh set of talks. At that point, however, it was far too late for second thoughts. The letter was broadcast from Baghdad on the morning of January 16. By then, the air war was already under way.

No Shelter from the Storm

Chapter 3

PUBLIC STATEMENTS MADE by Saddam before the air war began show a man strangely unconcerned about the damage superior coalition air forces could inflict on his precious war machine. At the same time, he was confident that the Iraqi air defense system would inflict heavy losses on coalition air forces. But once coalition warplanes entered Iraqi airspace and began dropping bombs and firing missiles, it was evident that he had made another major miscalculation: He had placed far too much confidence in Iraqi air defenses— and he had greatly underestimated the capabilities of coalition pilots and planes. His mistake created the momentum that led to the defeat of his ground forces a month later.

On paper, at least, the Iraqi air defense system was formidable. Its assets included eight hundred fighter planes, seven thousand radar-guided missiles, nine thousand missiles with infrared guidance, and at least seven thousand antiaircraft guns. In military parlance, the system was robust; it was also an integrated air defense system. In other words, all its guns, missiles, and planes were supposed to work in unison under a central command. Indeed, coalition planners feared that unless this sophisticated system could be destroyed, they would lose many planes. Baghdad was protected by the second-highest concentration of air defenses in the world. Only Moscow, the capital of the Soviet Union, was more heavily protected. The coalition's estimates for the number of losses it would incur during the first hours of combat ranged as high as fifty aircraft. Bush had been told to expect that about 3 percent of the hundreds of aircraft sent into Iraq that first night would not return.

Visible—or Invisible?

Before the air war began, coalition planners could not be sure that their Stealth fighter bombers were invisible to Iraqi radar. As described in *Triumph Without Victory,* a book compiled by the staff of *U.S. News & World Report,* Brigadier General C. Buster Glosson came up with a scheme that seemed to provide some answers:

> Most of the time, to check Iraqi reactions and see if they could pick up the F-117As, Glosson had had the Stealth pilots fly practice missions over Saudi territory and then return to the tankers. But on three occasions he had had the planes fly to within ten miles of the border and then fly another fifty miles up and down the border. On the second of these missions, Glosson tried something different. He had the F-117As turn on their transponders. . . . This way the Stealth fighters would appear on a radar screen, just like any conventional aircraft. With their transponders on, the F-117As had dashed toward the Iraqi border. Then, fifteen miles away, they had turned them off and gone into their Stealth mode of operation. To the Iraqi radar operators, it looked like ten fighters had headed right at them and then disappeared, probably dropping down under their radar beams. A day after this exercise, Baghdad accused the allies of overflying Iraq. In fact, the F-117As had turned away, never entering Iraqi airspace. The exercise had convinced Glosson that Stealth worked. If the Iraqi radar operators had seen the planes turn away, they would have never have broadcast their accusations.

When Time Stopped

Consequently, the mood was grim when, around midnight on January 16, hundreds of coalition aircraft took to the skies and headed into Iraq. At the command post in the basement of the Royal Saudi Air Force headquarters in Riyadh, men like Brigadier General C. Buster Glosson and Lieutenant General Chuck Horner watched events unfold on two giant radar screens. "Time kind of stood still," a navy officer in the command post recalled later, "as you saw those little dots moving toward Iraq."[42]

The primary objective that first night was to neutralize Iraqi defenses, either by attacking them directly or by disrupting the communication systems that connected Iraqi units with their commanders and allowed them to coordinate their fire. In order not to tip off the Iraqis that an attack was under way, all of the hundreds of missions were timed to reach their targets at about the same time—3:00 A.M. in Baghdad.

A row of U.S. Stealth fighters is ready for takeoff from a Saudi airfield. Stealth fighters were the first aircraft deployed to bomb key targets in Baghdad.

The night was moonless. This worked to the attackers' advantage because the Iraqi fighter pilots showed little enthusiasm for night flying and had rarely trained for it. Coalition planners hoped—correctly, as it turned out—that no Iraqi fighters would take to the skies. The darkness also made it harder for antiaircraft gunners to visually target attacking aircraft. In addition, Iraqi gunners had little time to prepare. Earlier that evening Apache attack helicopters had swept into Iraq and destroyed early warning radars just over the border. Other radar sites had been knocked out days before by Green Berets and other special forces teams secretly dropped inside the country.

Striking Out of the Night

Ten F-117 Stealth attack fighters, the bat-winged planes designed to be invisible to radar, had been assigned the mission of attacking targets in and around Baghdad. Because of the reputed sophisticaton of the Iraqi defenses, the airspace over the city was considered too dangerous for other types of aircraft. It seems that at least some Iraqi forces in Baghdad realized an attack was imminent. Even before coalition fighters arrived on the scene, antiaircraft gunners were firing into the sky. Major Jerry Leatherman piloted one of the attack fighters. In his book *Crusade: The Untold Story of the Persian Gulf War*, Rick Atkinson provided a colorful description of what Leatherman and his fellow Stealth pilots saw as they arrived in the airspace over Baghdad that first night:

> In vivid fountains of red and orange and gold, the enemy fire boiled up with an intensity that initially mesmerized more than it frightened. Missiles corkscrewed skyward or streaked up on white tubes of flame. Antiaircraft rounds—57mm, then 100mm —burst into hundreds of black and gray blossoms. Scarlet threads of gunfire stitched the air, woven so thickly as to suggest a solid sheet of fire—all the more alarming when Leatherman remembered that only every fifth round was a visible tracer. Yet for all its volume, the shooting seemed unguided; the Iraqis were flinging up random barrages in hopes of hitting something. . . . In effect, Leatherman realized, he was still invisible.[43]

At exactly 3:00 A.M. Leatherman dropped two two-thousand-pound laser-guided bombs on his first target, a twelve-story building in downtown Baghdad called the International Telephone Exchange. This structure was a critical target because the majority of military telecommunications in Iraq were routed through it. Leatherman's second bomb scored a direct hit, destroying the top four floors of the building in a blinding flash. After the explosion the skies over the city lit up with antiaircraft fire so intense that some pilots doubted they would survive the next few minutes.

A System in Shreds

Still, the coalition's pilots pressed on, hitting all of their assigned targets in less than fifteen minutes. By then, it was clear that Saddam's confidence in his air defense system was misplaced. Any radars still operating were failing to pinpoint the attackers. Although films of the attack show the skies lit up by tracers from antiaircraft guns, the gunners were simply firing blindly into the moonless night in hopes

Intense antiaircraft fire lights up the night sky over Baghdad as Iraqi forces try to repel the U.S.–led bombing attacks.

of making a lucky hit. None did. Among the targets hit and destroyed by coalition pilots in the first few hours were electric power plants; chemical, biological, and nuclear weapons plants; air defense sites; airfields; and missile launchers.

Captain Marcel Kerdavid was pleasantly surprised when, on their way back to Saudi Arabia, all ten of his fellow F-117 pilots checked in by radio. "I honestly didn't think we'd all make it home,"[44] he said. This unexpected level of success was repeated over and over again in the next few days. Meanwhile, the destruction of control centers in Baghdad and elsewhere meant that long-range early warning radars were of no use even if they survived the bombing. The country was now vulnerable to massive bombing raids. After that first night, as long as they remained at medium to high altitude, coalition bombers could safely fly almost anywhere in Iraq.

During the first twenty-four hours of the war, the coalition flew more than thirteen hundred sorties (missions by individual aircraft). At the same time, navy ships fired more than one hundred Tomahawk cruise missiles at Iraqi military targets. Although coalition war planners did not immediately realize it, in the first few hours of the war

---

 ## An Around-the-Clock War

In *From Shield to Storm,* military historians James F. Dunnigan and Austin Bay attributed the success of the coalition's air war to a combination of "high tech and high talent":

> The Gulf air war was notable for its around-the-clock nature, made possible by the large number of Allied aircraft equipped with sensors that allowed pilots to see anything at any time. Many of these same sensors, linked with powerful computers, vastly increased the accuracy of bombing, including so-called "dumb bombs." The iron "dumb bombs" dropped by coalition air forces during the conflict were in many cases nearly identical in design to the iron bombs used fifty years ago, but improved fire-control systems made them vastly more accurate.

> Success in the air war was expected; but *why* did the air war succeed so dramatically and prove to be so terribly decisive? High-technology equipment and pilot quality (top talent) are the two primary reasons.

---

they had severely crippled Iraq's air defense systems. Electronic communications were disrupted, some Iraqi commanders were killed, and dozens of air defense sites were destroyed. The poor performance of Iraq's expensive air defense system was a great shock to Saddam. In keeping with his customary practice, he expressed his displeasure by having its chief executed.

Blaming Subordinates

Saddam blamed the collapse of his air defense system on subordinates, but it was really a triumph of technology. The truth of the matter was that Iraqi defenses were no match for the sophisticated weapons the coalition had at its disposal. Some analysts have called the Gulf War "a true revolution in warfare."[45] The most successful air campaign in history made ample use of precision-guided weapons, stealth delivery systems, and advanced targeting systems. Because satellites provided both reconnaissance and communication, the Gulf War has also been called the first space war. Both satellites and airborne warning and control systems (AWACS) planes allowed coalition commanders to monitor exactly what was going on as it happened. *U.S. News & World Report* described the process as Glosson and Horner, both in the command center in Riyadh, anxiously watched the first night's attack unfold:

> As the first planes began departing their air bases, Glosson and Horner watched a large display screen at their headquarters in the basement of the Royal Saudi Air Force Headquarters building. The screen relayed information on the attack from an AWACS aircraft overhead. "The AWACS display was like a large TV screen in a bar for watching pro football," Horner said. "It goes from Israel to Teheran, from Turkey to Saudi Arabia. Everything that's flying appears on that screen except the Stealth [fighters]. And you might get a hit on [that is, see] a Stealth every now and then. I just sat there and watched planes take off and rendezvous."[46]

Invisible Planes and Tiny Televisions

The Stealth fighter was one of the technological stars of the war. Hundreds of missions were flown with no losses. Not only was it virtually invisible to Iraqi radar, but its precision bombs proved to be extremely accurate. The Tomahawk cruise missile was another

The USS Wisconsin *launches a cruise missile toward a Baghdad target. More than a hundred such missiles hit Iraqi targets during the first day of the war.*

relatively new weapon against which Iraq was defenseless. In *Crusade: The Untold Story of the Persian Gulf War*, Atkinson described how cruise missiles fired from navy ships in the Persian Gulf found their assigned targets on the first night of the war:

> The missiles from *Wisconsin* and her sister ships swept into Baghdad at nearly five hundred knots, heard but not seen. About eight miles from their targets, the Tomahawk's terrain-contour matching yielded to a different navigation system. Tiny television cameras clicked on and began scanning the landscape. . . .
>
> An optical sensor . . . scanned the passing scenery and divided the image into a matrix of black and white squares. Comparing the televised images with those stored in the Tomahawk's memory, a computer relayed commands to the missile's stubby wings and tail fins for final course adjustments.
>
> The first wave struck between 3:06 and 3:11 a.m. Eight missiles plowed into the presidential palace, their thousand-pound Bullpup warheads delaying for a few nanoseconds before erupting in a roar of flames and flying masonry. Six more hit the Baath Party headquarters compound. Thirty struck the vast missile complex at Taji, with a redundancy that reflected both the size of the target and lingering doubts about Tomahawk accuracy. Within twenty-four hours, 116 missiles would be fired from nine ships.[47]

Deception in the Dark

Even the rare successes of Iraqi antiaircraft crews ended up working against them. Decoy drones launched from bases in Saudi Arabia and from navy jets based on aircraft carriers drew attention away from the manned aircraft that were the real attack force. Programmed to fly in circles over Baghdad, the drones managed to stay in the air long enough to attract most of the antiaircraft fire. Many were eventually hit—one reason Iraqi gunners believed they had downed dozens of coalition planes.

All the attention focused on the drones exposed the antiaircraft system to further punishment. While the Iraqis were busy shooting down the drones, an armada of coalition planes fired high-speed missiles with 145-pound warheads designed to follow radar beams back to their point of origin and destroy the radar facility. That first night, coalition planes launched two hundred antiradar missiles. Like the laser-guided bombs, most of them found their targets.

"That's probably one of the main reasons why I was only able to use the drones that once," reported Glosson, who was one of the planners of the air war. "They wouldn't turn on their radars anymore."[48] Radars that were never turned on, however, were of little use to Saddam's air defense system. The net effect was to paralyze Saddam's antiaircraft assets.

A Paradise for Planes

Regarding the air war, military historians James F. Dunnigan and Austin Bay noted that there were other factors working against Saddam—factors that had nothing to do with technology. In their book *From Shield to Storm*, they pointed out that the geography of Iraq was a dream come true for combat aircraft:

> The terrain in the Persian Gulf is nearly ideal for offensive air operations. This is because it's relatively flat and contains little vegetation for the enemy to hide in. The terrain is also dry, so cutting ground forces off from their supplies has more impact because the loss of water supplies is more damaging than any other supply problem. Ironically, Iraq was the area where air operations in the desert were first tested and perfected by the British Royal Air Force in the 1920s and 1930s.[49]

Ineffective Iraqi Fighters

With so much of his radar destroyed and his missiles and antiaircraft guns rendered ineffective, Saddam had to depend on his eight hundred fighter planes to ward off coalition aircraft. But their performance turned out to be another major disappointment. Even his modern F-1 Mirage fighters, equipped with deadly Exocet missiles, were ineffective. During the entire war, not one successful Iraqi air attack against coalition ground or naval forces was recorded. Iraqi aircraft did try to intercept coalition aircraft in the early days of the war. The authors of *Desert Storm: The Gulf War and What We Learned*, described a typical encounter. Two F-18 fighters had just taken off from the carrier *Saratoga* and were heading into Iraq when an AWACS plane alerted them to the approach of two unidentified planes:

Smart Bombs Were Not Always Smart

Some of the most dramatic moments of the war, from the public's standpoint, were briefings in Riyadh or Washington where films of laser-guided bombs perfectly hitting their targets were shown. As Rick Atkinson points out in *Crusade: The Untold Story of the Persian Gulf War,* these "smart bombs" were not nearly as accurate as portrayed:

> Thousands of feet of gun camera video tape of bombs missing their targets remained classifed; only flawless missions displaying dead-on accuracy were released—with the audio recordings of cursing, hyperventilating pilots primly excised. Of 167 laser-guided bombs dropped during the first five nights of combat by F-117s, considered the most accurate aircraft system in the allied arsenal, seventy-six missed their targets because of pilot error, mechanical or electronic malfunctions, or poor weather. None of those was acknowledged by Riyadh or Washington.

A technician prepares the fuses on a "smart bomb." The accuracy of such bombs was greatly exaggerated.

The two groups of planes were closing at a combined speed of more than 1,300 miles per hour.

Each of the F-18 pilots locked his radar onto one of the Iraqi planes. . . . They decided to let the approaching planes come to within visual range before firing to make certain they were indeed enemy. When the Iraqi planes—MiG-21s, as it turned out—could be seen, the U.S. pilots quickly checked for the telltale smoke or other signals that the Iraqis might be firing missiles. They were not. . . .

After what seemed like a lifetime to the U.S. pilots, they finally decided to fire. Sparrow air-to-air missiles streaked out from their wings. The shot was a tough one. When aircraft are closing head-on, the high intercept speed and small target presented by an approaching plane create difficulties for heat-seeking or radar-guided missiles. But the Sparrows found their mark, and both Iraqi planes exploded and crashed to the ground.[50]

Thirty-five Iraqi fighters were shot down in air-to-air combat during the first days of the war. Coalition forces, by comparison, experienced no air-to-air combat losses during the entire war. After the initial one-sided encounters, Iraqi planes essentially sat out the rest of the war. Eventually, about 150 of them flew to Iran. The reason for these flights was not clear, but according to one defense analyst, "It seems likely that individual pilots, and then entire groups, had decided that their chances of survival were minimal: their choices seemed to be suicide by air-to-air combat or execution by Saddam Hussein or his security forces."[51] In the end, the billions of dollars Saddam had spent to build the world's sixth-largest air force did him little good.

Saddam's Secret Weapon

But Saddam had one last weapon that he believed would turn the war to his advantage: the Scud missile. These missiles, which had been purchased some years earlier from the Soviet Union, were not particularly accurate and did not do enough damage to be of any great military value. Saddam knew, however, they would have great political impact. Every Scud that fell on Saudi Arabia would show that the coalition was unable to protect the kingdom and perhaps lead Saudis to question their government's decision to go to war against Iraq.

It was Israel's response, however, that Saddam was counting on to turn the tide in his favor. Eight Scuds were fired at targets in Israel on the second night of the war—six fell on Tel Aviv and two on Haifa. Saddam was certain Israel would retaliate against him militarily—its stated national policy called for immediate retaliation against any attacker. If Israel did retaliate, Saddam was convinced that the Arab nations in the coalition would refuse to fight alongside their hated enemy.

The Scud Strategy

Saddam's plans to split the coalition depended on attacking Israel, a strategy he felt sure would lead to retaliation by the Israelis. In their book *Saddam Hussein: A Political Biography,* Efraim Karsh and Inari Rautsi tell how the Scuds fired at them by Saddam placed the Israelis in an awkward, unfamiliar position:

> An indication that Israel was indeed an integral component of Saddam's war strategy had already been given during the first day of the war, when the Iraqi Ambassador to Belgium, Ziad Haidar, revealed that the decision to attack Israel had been taken and that such an attack was imminent. Before long Haidar's promise was made good: in the early-morning hours of January 18, three Iraqi ballistic missiles landed in Tel Aviv and two in the northern port city of Haifa.

> Though causing few fatalities the attacks punctured the bubble of euphoria in the coalition following the initial air offensive, and aroused apprehensions of an Israeli response. The Israelis themselves were disconcerted. For the first time since the establishment of their state, its main population centers had come under indiscriminate attack by a regular Arab army. No less frustrating for the Israelis was the painful awareness that they had been "hijacked" into a war that was not theirs, without being able to do anything about it. Retaliation, one of the main foundations of Israel's strategic thinking over the past four decades, seemed to offer no solution to the newly posed challenge. The underlying logic of retaliation had been to deter attacks against Israel by impressing upon would-be aggressors that their losses were bound to exceed any potential gains. Yet, this rationale was completely irrelevant to this situation, for no reason other than that Saddam's aggression was designed to trigger a response, not to avoid one.

Iraqi Scud missiles leveled these buildings in downtown Tel Aviv, Israel. Saddam fired on Israeli targets in an unsuccessful bid to draw Israel into the Gulf War.

Analysts acknowledge that had Israel responded by attacking Iraq, it might well have split the coalition. Indeed, as the Scuds began hitting Israel, there was near panic in Washington—particularly when the first reports from Tel Aviv erroneously reported that the Scuds there had released nerve gas. For a few hours it seemed as if events were about to spin out of control. "If they've been hit with chemicals, Katie bar the door because they're going to do something," said Deputy Secretary of State Lawrence Eagleburger. "I know these people. They're going to retaliate. If it's nerve gas, we'll never stop them."[52]

Diplomacy Saves the Day

The situation seemed even more desperate when U.S. military leaders learned that more than sixty Israeli warplanes had roared into the night. No one knew for sure whether they were heading for Iraq or just being scrambled against a possible attack. Secretary of State James

Baker, however, was able to defuse the situation with some hasty phone calls to Israeli prime minister Yitzhak Shamir. He promised that the coalition would do their absolute best to find and take out the Scud launchers. And he was able to convince the Israeli leader that immediate retaliation would not be in his country's best interest.

Israel's eventual decision not to enter the war doomed Saddam's chances of splitting the coalition. Although Scuds were fired up until the end of the war—eighty-six were launched in all—only one of them did major damage. The seventy-first Scud killed twenty-eight soldiers when it landed on a converted army barracks in Dhahran, Saudi Arabia. Meanwhile, the air war was going far better than anyone had predicted. Two weeks into the war, so many Iraqi command centers had been destroyed that Saddam was forced to run the war from inadequate facilities in mobile command vehicles.

Air superiority over Iraq and Kuwait was established so quickly that coalition forces soon turned their attention toward Iraqi forces on the ground. Disrupting the supply lines was a high priority; therefore, most railroad and highway bridges were attacked. According to the U.S. Department of Defense, thirty-three of thirty-six targeted highway and railroad bridges were bombed successfully, further isolating Iraqi forces. The amount of supplies reaching Kuwait was reduced from twenty thousand to two thousand tons per day.

Killing Tanks the Easy Way

Air attacks then turned to individual targets such as tanks and artillery pieces. Technology again worked against Saddam as coalition commanders came up with an ingenious way to kill Iraqi tanks. Buried in the sand, with sandbags placed on top, these tanks were difficult to find and dangerous to bomb because aircraft had to swoop in low to drop bombs accurately. As they did so, they were vulnerable to anti-aircraft and even small arms fire.

Then someone discovered that the Iraqis liked to keep the tanks' engines running at night in order to provide warmth and power. In addition, the tanks were metal, and absorbed heat during the day. Using F-111s equipped with infrared detectors and laser-guided bombs, the coalition forces found that they could easily "see" and kill the tanks at night from a safe altitude. Suddenly, finding and bombing camouflaged

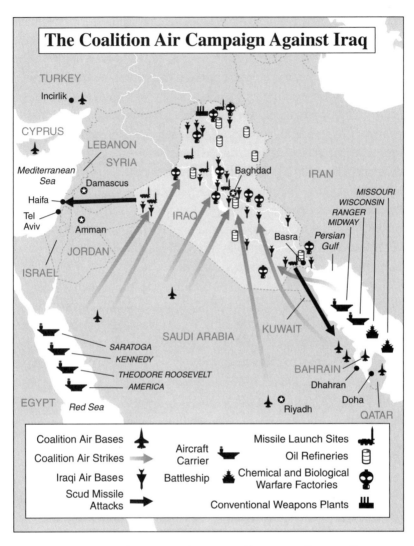

The Coalition Air Campaign Against Iraq

tanks was no longer dangerous. As reported in *Desert Storm*, pilots came up with a nickname for this novel method of tank killing: "Pilots soon coined a phrase for the tactic—'tank plinking'—and with this tactic, air force units were 'reportedly destroying 100 to 150 Iraqi tanks per day before the ground war started.'"[53]

A Defenseless Nation

The failure of Saddam's air defenses paved the way for the defeat of his forces in Kuwait and was a disaster for Iraq and its people. Elaine

Sciolino, a correspondent for the *New York Times*, summed up the plight of a country that had no way to protect itself from aerial attack:

Night after night, awed planes and missiles relentlessly pounded Saddam's troops and systematically destroyed his country's military infrastructure. In one month of war—the most intense aerial bombardment in military history—the allied coalition flew about 100,000 sorties, an average of one bombing mission a minute. The allies demolished most of Iraq's strategic sites, including command-and-control centers, factories, ministries, Baath Party headquarters, bridges, power stations, and various other targets. They also destroyed the bulk of Saddam's tanks, armor and artillery; demoralized the Army; and terrorized his people. . . . An Iraqi man quoted by Reuters news agency in a February dispatch could have been speaking for the Iraqi nation when he said, "The Americans inflicted more damage on our country in two hours than the Iranians did in eight years."[54]

The Mother
Chapter 4 of All Retreats

I N THE MONTHS leading up to the Gulf War, Saddam warned the world that if his troops in Kuwait were attacked, they would inflict casualties so heavy that coalition forces would be forced into a humiliating retreat. He referred to the coming ground war as the "Mother of All Battles." The reality would turn out to be far different. When the ground war came, Saddam's troops gave a very poor account of themselves—and the fault lay squarely with their leaders.

As an attack by coalition ground forces loomed, Saddam sought to demonstrate what they were in for by mounting an attack on the Saudi coastal town of Khafji. The town's twenty thousand residents had abandoned Khafji when the war began. It was protected by a small group of Saudi soldiers. Rather than terrorizing coalition forces, however, the operation provided the first indication that Iraq's troops were not as fearsome as they had been made out to be.

Saddam personally planned the surprise attack on Khafji. His purpose was not to hold the town for long—the real aim was to draw a large force of U.S. Marines into the town, where they would be pinned down and destroyed. Had it worked, the plan would have undoubtedly been a big morale booster for the Iraqis. Unfortunately for Saddam, the attack had the opposite effect from the one he intended.

An Attack Gone Awry

Saddam's battle plan involved a three-pronged attack on the town. First, a force of about forty-five tanks from the 5th Mechanized Division, one of Saddam's most highly regarded units, crossed the border and drove down the coastal road toward Khafji. Such a heavy armored force would have little trouble with the few Saudis defending the town (and, in fact, the Saudis were quickly driven out). Saddam believed that U.S. Marines would then try to retake the town. He hoped to crush them between Iraqi tank forces moving in from the west and other Iraqi forces that had secretly infiltrated the area from the sea to the east. The attack began in the predawn hours of January 30. Because of satellite and aerial surveillance, the Iraqi movements were no surprise to the coalition commanders. They were actually able to count all the approaching vehicles in each of the three separate attacks.

Almost immediately, the plan unraveled. Soon after crossing the border, the westernmost Iraqi forces unexpectedly collided with the 1st Marine Division and a running gun battle developed. The marines' lightly armored vehicles were never designed to engage with heavy battle tanks, but they discovered that their night-vision sights allowed them to fire at and destroy Iraqi tanks from a safe distance. Many other enemy tanks were killed by aircraft, and these Iraqi forces eventually retreated. The Iraqi seaborne forces, meanwhile, were intercepted and destroyed long before they reached Khafji.

The Iraqis controlled Khafji for only about thirty-six hours. They were driven out on January 31 in a counterattack by Saudi and Qatari forces supported by U.S. Marine artillery and air power. An unforeseen

---

A U.S. Marine takes up a position near the town of Khafji. U.S. troops quickly drove Saddam's forces from the coastal town.

An Iraqi armored vehicle outside Khafji smolders after being hit. Iraqi armor proved particularly vulnerable to antitank missiles and aerial assault.

consequence of the Khafji offensive was that coalition commanders gained valuable insight into how vulnerable Iraqi armor was to antitank missiles and aerial attack.

The abortive operation also revealed another Iraqi weakness: Morale among the troops was low. Some of the four hundred Iraqis who surrendered claimed that they had advanced into battle only at the point of their officers' guns. Furthermore, many of the Iraqi vehicles that were destroyed had been abandoned first—a telling sign that what was supposedly a good Iraqi army unit lacked the will to fight. The poor performance must have discouraged the Iraqis. Lieutenant Colonel Thomas Strauss of the 1st Armored Division noted, "When you send in the 5th Mech and they get drubbed, it's got to have an effect on the rest of your units."[55]

Valuable Lessons

Coalition forces, on the other hand, gained confidence. Not only were the Iraqis much less fearsome than first thought, but the quality of their leadership was questionable. For example, the failure to coordinate the offensive properly—many units never reached their attack positions—was a sign that the command structure was too rigid to adjust to changing circumstances. Each unit seemed to follow its preset agenda regardless of the military consequences. In all likelihood, officers were afraid of the consequences of deviating from Saddam's original plan.

Other weaknesses were also apparent. Some Iraqi units were unable to find their way safely back across the border through their own minefields, a sign of either poor navigation skills or inadequate communication between units. The defense of Kuwait would be much more difficult if the Iraqis were not sure where they had laid their own mines. In theory, the mines should have been laid in such a way that they would funnel an attacking force into an area where they could be decimated by artillery fire. But the fact that the Iraqis seemed unable to adjust their artillery fire to hit forces on the move was another encouraging sign for the coalition.

The attack on Khafji came with a high price tag. Hundreds of Iraqi soldiers were killed and about eighty Iraqi tanks were destroyed outside the town or along the border. The U.S. Marines lost a total of eleven men in the fighting—and seven of those died in a "friendly fire" incident when a U.S. Air Force A-10 mistakenly bombed a marine light armored vehicle. Nevertheless, Saddam announced a great victory. The announcement merely served to reveal another weakness in the Iraqi chain of command. As defense analyst Norman Friedman explained, "He proclaimed success, not so much because he needed a victory to boost public morale, but because without any evidence he really assumed that his plan had won."[56]

Saddam's lack of knowledge about what was really going on further encouraged coalition commanders. It was clear that accurate information was not reaching him from the front. Given his past record, Iraqi military commanders would have been extremely reluctant to give Saddam bad news. His ignorance also seemed to extend to knowledge of the whereabouts of American units. Captured Iraqi soldiers, for example, expressed surprise at finding U.S. forces so near the border. Their astonishment suggested to coalition planners that the deceptions planned as an integral part of the coming ground war had a good chance of success.

The author of *Crusade: The Untold Story of the Gulf War* summed up the lessons of Khafji this way:

More important, the battle cut the Iraqis down to size. A credible battle plan had been executed badly by enemy troops who lacked air power, the ability to adjust artillery fire, even the wherewithal to avoid their own obstacle belts when forced to retreat. Allied warplanes riddled a number of tanks and trucks trapped between two minefields north of Khafji. [U.S. general Norman] Schwartzkopf later estimated that 80 percent of the Iraqi 5th Mechanized division had been obliterated. The enemy also lacked the fire in the belly required, in military vernacular, to close with and destroy their foe.[57]

Iraq's Formidable Edge

Despite the poor showing of his forces at Khafji, Saddam had a huge advantage as he prepared to defend Kuwait. Intelligence estimates suggested that Iraq had twice as many combat soldiers as the coalition did—about a half million troops in all. Dug in behind minefields, trenches, and fixed artillery, they represented a formidable force. Compared to the coalition, they also had more weapons on the ground. The Iraqis had more tanks (forty-seven hundred versus thirty-five hundred) and more artillery pieces. Saddam had little doubt that he would inflict heavy casualties on anyone trying to evict him from Kuwait.

But the system he used to communicate with his frontline troops had serious flaws. "Command and control" is the phrase by which military experts refer to such systems. The best of these provide a central commander with accurate, up-to-date knowledge of developments on a battlefield. They allow him to realize an army's full potential by moving troops and weapons to wherever they are needed most.

Good command and control systems require good communication networks, but after a month of coalition bombing, Saddam did not have one. Given this development, a wise alternative would have been to decentralize authority and let officers in the field make their own decisions. Saddam rejected this strategy. As always, he feared that rivals might rise up if given any real power. Instead, he chose the worst possible option: He alone made decisions—and those decisions were often based on faulty or incomplete information.

The Iraqi leader had only himself to blame for the poor information he received. As he had during the Iran-Iraq War, Saddam sent his poorest, least loyal troops to the front lines. Behind them he placed

A Scheme to Discourage Desertions?

In his book *Desert Victory,* Norman Friedman mentions a strategy employed by the Iraqis that may have been designed to prevent their front-line troops from surrendering:

> The attack on Khafji itself included an element of deception, apparently planned by the attacking brigade. For some time Iraqi troops had been heavily leafletted from the air. They were called upon to surrender. In the case of tanks, the intention to surrender would be signaled by approaching with the turret reversed. In this case the Iraqi tanks approached the Saudi and Qatari special forces troops on the border with their turrets pointed backwards. The accompanying Iraqi infantry had their hands up. As soon as the Saudis emerged from their foxholes to accept the defectors, the tanks turned their turrets around and opened fire. The Iraqi infantry drew weapons from their boots and they also began to fire.
>
> It was never entirely clear whether this deception was intended as more than an attempt to gain a temporary advantage. There was some speculation that its real purpose was to convince coalition troops to fire upon future Iraqi defectors. The Iraqi leadership may have reasoned that word of such incidents, passed within the Iraqi lines, would convince troops that defection was pointless. Certainly there was later abundant evidence that, almost from the first, the Iraqi leadership feared that its troops would bolt.

tactical reserves. Even further back, inside Iraq, were his best and most loyal troops—the Republican Guard. Saddam considered his frontline troops expendable, but a consequence of putting such inexperienced troops at the forefront of the battle was that he was not able to get accurate reports on enemy movements. Even Iraqi troops lucky enough to escape and make it back to the rear were rarely knowledgeable enough to give accurate reports to more able military commanders.

Troops Let Down

Failure to realize or take into account his troops' lack of morale and motivation may have been Saddam's biggest shortcoming. In the last days before the fighting actually began, many regular army officers actually abandoned their units. The remaining troops knew they were expendable and therefore had little incentive to fight. Huddled in trenches and bunkers, often reduced to eating a handful of rice a day, they were not mentally or physically ready to fight. Hassam Malek Mohammad Mardy's poor morale was typical. Shortly before he was killed by coalition bullets he confided his despair in his diary:

> I am like a prisoner. My stomach is sick. I live unhappy, alone, all day long. May God make this problem easy. May it be solved quickly. . . . I open my eyes and cry, sitting, thinking, "Oh God, will you accept me?" I close my eyes and remember. Then I cry again. There is sand on my face. It is about to cover me. It is my destiny.[58]

The Perfect Preparation

While Saddam sent his most poorly trained soldiers to the front lines, coalition soldiers on the other side of the border were exceptionally well prepared. Many, in essence, had trained for this war in advance. Air force, marine, and navy pilots all had practiced in the deserts of the American West. And the army and marines had conducted huge

Iraqi soldiers surrender to coalition forces in Kuwait. Low morale drove a large number of Iraqi troops to surrender to coalition forces.

mock battles in California's Mojave Desert. Many of the tactics developed there would be used effectively against Iraq. By comparison, the Iraqis were not particularly skilled in desert warfare, despite their eight-year war with neighboring Iran. That conflict had been fought, not in the desert, but on mostly marshy terrain in southeast Iraq and western Iran.

Deception Was Crucial

This time the fighting would indeed happen in the desert, but not where the Iraqis were expecting. The coalition battle plan was to deceive Saddam into thinking the main attack was coming through Kuwait. Meanwhile, armored forces would maneuver quickly behind the Iraqis, threatening to cut them off from Baghdad. A huge armored force of about a quarter of a million men and more than one thousand tanks near the Kuwait border were secretly moved an average of two hundred miles to the west. That armored force was designed to slice deep into Iraq and then turn east to slam into the Iraqi army's flank north of Kuwait. The maneuver would force the Iraqis to come out of their dug-in defenses or risk being completely cut off. In doing so, they would become much more vulnerable to coalition armor, artillery, and aircraft. As General Colin Powell said of the Iraqi army, "First we are going to cut it off and then we are going to kill it."[59]

Instead of liberating Kuwait with a direct—and costly—assault, General Norman Schwartzkopf had decided that the main objective should be the destruction of the Iraqi army. He assumed that once the army was destroyed, Kuwait would be freed. A key to the success of his plan was the freezing of Iraqi units in place in Kuwait so that they could not react in time to the huge force moving in on them from the west.

Once again, Saddam was in the dark, thanks to deceptions that were used to create the impression that the main attack was coming through Kuwait. In the Persian Gulf, for example, eighteen thousand U.S. Marines boarded ships, suggesting that an amphibious invasion of Kuwait was imminent. The threat from the sea tied down six Iraqi divisions along the coast. Farther inland, phantom units broadcast thousands of phony radio messages. Dummy tanks and artillery pieces were built and prerecorded tank sounds were played loudly over audio systems.

The Iraqis had little opportunity to uncover such ruses. Saddam had no satellites to provide intelligence and coalition aircraft made sure no Iraqi pilots got off the ground to see what was really going on. The Iraqis remained unaware that hundreds of thousands of coalition troops had moved far to the west.

Meanwhile, coalition forces conducted a number of operations along the border that were intended to convince Saddam that the main attack would come through Kuwait. Military historians James F. Dunnigan and Austin Bay discussed the importance of these feints in their book *From Shield to Storm:*

> Attacks occurred regularly from February 15 through February 21. Lots of artillery was used. Allied casualties were light; Iraqi losses were much heavier. . . . The Iraqis were left with the impression that American forces would attack into the Iraqi lines. This maneuver (and the USMC [United States Marine Corps] coastal exercises) "sold" the Iraqis on the idea of a U.S. attack into the teeth of their defenses. Iraqi reserves (mechanized and armored divisions) thus prepared to move south instead of west to meet this "main allied attack." The importance of the feint operations cannot be underestimated. The ruse worked, as the Iraqis continued to prepare for Allied frontal attacks, which made the "swing to the west" all the more effective.[60]

The Ground War Begins

Bush set a deadline of noon on February 22 for Iraq to begin its withdrawal from Kuwait, or face a ground attack that would utterly destroy his army. The deadline passed, and at 4 A.M. on Sunday, February 24, coalition ground forces attacked along a three-hundred-mile front. To preserve the illusion of the main attack coming through Kuwait, coalition Arab forces and U.S. units moved into Kuwait at three points. In the far west the army's 1st Cavalry and Arab units made a feint toward the Wadi Al-Batin, a dry riverbed that would have been a natural avenue for an armored force. Their actions held another four Iraqi infantry divisions in place.

Along the Persian Gulf, Arab forces under Saudi command began fighting their way up the coastal road toward Kuwait City. To their west the 1st and 2nd Marine divisions and the army's Tiger Brigade faced the most dangerous combinations of minefields and defensive obstacles. They had to find a passage through belts of antitank and

Meals Ready to Not Eat

With several hundred thousand troops living in the desert, hot meals were not always available. Instead, soldiers had to make do with prepackaged meals called MREs ("meals ready to eat"). Molly Moore, a correspondent with the *Washington Post,* accompanied the marines into Kuwait. Her account of what she saw, a book called *A Woman at War,* makes clear that most soldiers did not look forward to their MREs:

> When I'd first arrived in Saudi Arabia, an Army private asked me if I knew what MRE meant. "Sure," I replied. "Meals Ready to Eat."
>
> "No, ma'am," countered the private. "Meals Rejected by Ethiopians."
>
> Whatever they were called, I—along with thousands of troops in Saudi Arabia—detested the modern-day military replacement for C rations. The meals, packaged in unappetizing dirt-brown plastic pouches, came in a variety of menus, ranging from freeze-dried pork patties with the consistency of Styrofoam to packets of chicken a la king with the smell and appearance of expensive cat food. I usually ate little more than the crackers with squeezable packets of peanut butter or cheese and the dessert, crumbly brownies or stale fruit nut cake.

antipersonnel mines. They managed to do so by using rocket-propelled mine-clearing charges, special ropelike tubes filled with explosives. Flung across a minefield and detonated, they set off the mines and cleared a path.

Light Resistance

Meanwhile, Iraqi artillery was not as numerous or as accurate as coalition planners had feared. Within a half hour the character of the battle was becoming apparent. Iraqi resistance was light and thousands of enemy troops could not wait to surrender. Wave after wave abandoned their positions. The coalition bombing, as well as neglect by Iraqi leaders, had taken a heavy toll on morale. More than a few front-line troops were starving and lice ridden. By the end of the day, at least five thousand had surrendered. They claimed that with their officers and Baath Party officials gone, they had planned on giving up at the first opportunity. Some even showed coalition troops how to safely navigate through the minefields.

Prince Khalid bin Sultan, the Saudi general who commanded the Arab forces, had this to say of the Iraqis: "I'm not underestimating the Iraqi soldiers' ability and professionalism in fighting . . . . But there is one thing they are lacking, that they don't believe what they are fighting for right now."[61]

There were a number of other reasons the Iraqi defenses were lacking. Trenches filled with oil were not set on fire, mines were not buried completely, and artillery fire was absent or inaccurate. Still, things could have been very different had the Iraqis been motivated to fight.

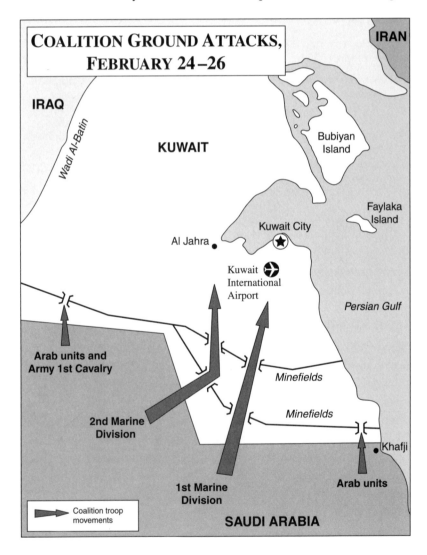

"We were very much impressed with the defensive abilities that the Iraqis had set up," said Sergeant Robert Novak, leader of an antitank missile squad in the 2nd Marine Division. "If they had not withdrawn, it would have been very, very hard."[62]

An All-Out Attack

One of the reasons coalition troops met so little resistance was the successful use of the AirLand Battle doctrine. This plan of attack called for simultaneous strikes by aircraft, missiles, and long-range artillery against potential reinforcements for enemy troops battling on the front lines. Designed to overwhelm and demoralize an enemy, it worked exceptionally well against Iraqi troops, who were not willing to die for Kuwait in the first place.

Lieutenant Bill Delaney of the 1st Marine Division was commander of one of the first tanks to breach Iraqi defenses in Kuwait. Molly Moore the author of *A Woman at War*, went along with the 1st Marines. She reported what Delaney saw after passing through the first mine belt:

> Delaney sat on the lip of the commander's hatch, chewing an MRE and listening to the artillery shells whistle over his head toward the Iraqi defensive line north of the second minefield that stretched before him. Delaney figured that his men had had it easy in the first obstacle belt. Here, they would meet the full force of the Iraqi defensive front.
>
> As Delaney's gaze wandered idly over the plains in front of him, he spotted a head pop up from the ground. He ordered McKee [his gunner] to train the gun on the hole. The head disappeared. A new barrage of artillery thundered overhead. Suddenly fifteen Iraqi troops burst out of the hole, waving white flags and marching in single file toward Delaney's platoon.[63]

Those fifteen were some of the thousands who surrendered from their trenches. Others abandoned their artillery emplacements and tanks. In the relatively few instances where Iraqi tanks stood and fought, coalition tanks proved far superior. But many more Iraqi tanks were destroyed long before they could reach the battlefield. The most effective aircraft against Iraqi tanks was the A-10 Warthog. On the second day of the ground war Captain Eric Salomonson and 1st Lieutenant

John Marks set a remarkable record. In three sorties and nine hours of flying they managed to destroy twenty-three enemy tanks—seventeen with heat-seeking missiles and six with their 30 mm machine guns. "It was an A-10 driver's dream,"[64] recalled Salomonson. The achievement was even more impressive because it was made amidst fog and heavy smoke from the six hundred oil wells the Iraqis had set ablaze.

Saddam Changes His Mind

Despite the poor visibility, the coalition achieved almost all its objectives during its first two days fighting inside Kuwait. The biggest problem, in fact, was what to do with all the surrendering Iraqis. In some areas coalition troops had to stop taking prisoners because doing so was slowing them down too much. They just tossed the Iraqis food and water and kept on moving.

By the morning of February 26, the 1st Marine Division had secured Kuwait International Airport, just southwest of Kuwait City. Later that day, as the extent of the destruction of Iraqi forces become obvious even to him, Saddam went on the radio to declare a moral victory. To the relief of coalition forces, who had feared house-to-house fighting inside Kuwait City, he also announced a complete withdrawal from Kuwait.

This announcement was not enough to satisfy Bush, who warned that only soldiers who laid down their equipment and arms would be safe from attack. Even before Saddam's announcement, however, his army was displaying a lack of professionalism and discipline that served only to make the punishment from coalition forces more severe. Troops fled Kuwait City in a panic. More than a thousand vehicles—including tanks, armored personnel carriers, and stolen cars, buses, and trucks—jammed the four-lane highway leading north to Iraq. The vehicles were loaded not only with soldiers, but with ample evidence of their looting. They carried televisions, video recorders, jewelry, perfume, clothing, and even toys.

The looters did not get far. Bush was determined that the Iraqis would pay dearly for ravaging Kuwait. Coalition air attacks hammered the mile-long convoy, effectively halting it by disabling the vehicles at the head and rear. The rest of the vehicles were destroyed in what some pilots called a turkey shoot. They left a burning mass of tangled, twisted wreckage.

Dinosaurs on the Prowl

In *Desert Storm*, the authors described what may have been the last armed encounter inside Kuwait. The army's Tiger Brigade, with forty-five of its Abrams M1A1 tanks, had been sent north to Mutala Ridge to try to catch the rear of Iraqi forces retreating from Kuwait City:

> A *Newsweek* reporter riding with the 2nd Brigade described the M1A1s "like nothing so much as great dinosaurs sniffing for prey ... their big 120 mm guns swinging restlessly from side to side." Driving at twenty-five miles per hour along the highway, the brigade scattered the few Iraqi forces before it, not even stopping to pick up prisoners. "Huddled groups of green-uniformed soldiers waving white rags of surrender stood, bewildered, while tanks roared by." The brigade reached Mutala around 4 P.M. and immediately attacked the rearguard of the Iraqi forces. For the next several minutes, U.S. armored troops were engaged in a wild melee with Iraqi T-55s. After the short but intense

Three Corsair bombers position themselves to bomb Iraqi tanks. Coalition bombers destroyed many Iraqi tanks before they reached the battlefield.

Trashing Kuwait on the Way Out

The Iraqis did not leave Kuwait gracefully. In what might best be described as an act of national vandalism, they did as much damage to the country as they possibly could. Elaine Sciolino tallied some of the destruction in her book *The Outlaw State:*

> As the Iraqi soldiers fled, they torched 600 of the country's 950 oil wells, creating towering fires and choking black smoke that dimmed the sun all the way from northern Saudi Arabia to central Iran, produced soot-contaminated "black rain" and threatened to change the weather patterns of the entire Gulf Region. Unexploded mines littered beaches and the highway to Baghdad; food, water, medical supplies, and gasoline were scarce; and much of the emirate was without electricity and phone service. Before leaving, the Iraqis shelled hotels and government buildings, and burned the National Assembly headquarters. Much of the emir's Dasman Palace was destroyed, its rooms gutted, its hallways smeared with human excrement.

Kuwaiti oil wells burn behind an Iraqi tank. Retreating Iraqis deliberately set fire to the wells.

firefight, the 22nd Brigade succeeded in overwhelming the Iraqi rearguard, which abandoned its tanks and fled into the desert.[65]

Saddam's "Mother of All Battles" was turning out far different than he had predicted. But his best troops had yet to enter the fray. But they, too, would suffer the consequences of Saddam's failings.

Ambush in the
Chapter 5 Desert

W

HILE SADDAM'S FORCES inside Kuwait were being routed, an even nastier surprise was about to be sprung on his more experienced and better equipped units in southern Iraq. Military units of any kind are at their most vulnerable when attacked from the side. Accordingly, perhaps the most basic rule of warfare is for commanders to never let the enemy outflank them. Yet that is exactly what happened to Saddam's Republican Guard—his best equipped and most heavily armed divisions. By ignoring basic military doctrine, the Iraqis set themselves up for the most devastating surprise attack in the history of tank warfare.

Blame for the failure went all the way up to Saddam, whose war plan made no allowances for such an event. Tom Carhart, author of *Iron Soldiers*, a history of the 1st Armored Division's participation in the war, explained how Saddam had layered his defenses in the unwavering belief that the main coalition attack would come through Kuwait:

> The frontline Iraqi troops were infantry divisions, with some modest armor to strengthen their line. These troops were understrength, and consisted mostly of poorly trained draftees. Neither the Iraqis nor the Americans expected them to stop or even really seriously hinder an American invasion. But right behind them were their reserves, an array of fourteen armored and mechanized divisions, some armed with the hot T-72 Soviet tank. These reserves could be expected to counterattack the invading American forces.

The coup de grace, Saddam Hussein believed, would be delivered against the Allied forces by six Republican Guard divisions, three armored and three infantry, that were still in Iraq, dug in and protected in deep reserve just north and northwest of the Kuwaiti border. After the fourteen reserve Iraqi divisions had counterattacked, bled, and stopped the invading Allies, these Republican Guard divisions would fall on them and destroy them.[66]

Searching for an Alternative

Coalition war planners, however, were determined not to follow Saddam's script. They began to look for a way around the Iraqis' entrenched defenses. Those defenses extended roughly sixty miles west of the tri-border area, where Iraq, western Kuwait, and Saudi Arabia come together. Saddam assumed that the rough desert beyond this point would be impassable for an invasion force. In the beginning coalition planners agreed with him. As Carhart noted, "The whole area, running far to the west and covering an area that went forty to fifty kilometers north into Iraq from the Saudi border, was broken ground littered by huge boulders and split by steep-sided gullies and ravines, clearly 'no go' territory for tanks at first glance."[67]

Then intelligence officers took a closer look at the area. Scouting expeditions by special forces troops, satellite photos, and airborne reconnaissance missions all suggested that a way might be found through the desert. Of particular significance was the fact, overlooked by Saddam, that the Bedouin tribesmen in the area traveled in pickup trucks. As one image analyst explained to Lieutenant General Frederick M. Franks Jr., commander of VII Corps, "It may be rough going . . . for wheeled vehicles, but it's definitely passable; you can tell that from all the tire tracks throughout the area."[68] Given the almost complete lack of Iraqi defenses farther west, passage through the boulder fields and then out onto the flatter terrain farther north seemed a better alternative than trying to fight through the entrenched defenses along the Kuwait border.

Safe Passage or Trap?

Still, this flanking maneuver was a gamble. Major General Ronald Griffith, commander of the 1st Armored Division, had a recurring nightmare

Coalition tanks roll across the Saudi desert toward Iraq. Saddam thought the desert would prevent coalition forces from outflanking his Republican Guard.

in which he would have to call Franks with bad news the day after the ground attack began:

> Hey, boss, I guess I misread the maps and the photo imagery, and made the wrong assumptions, because now it looks like your corps staff was right: We can't get through this terrain, it's really impassable for armored vehicles, and, oh, by the way, now that we tried and failed, the 1st Armored Division is stuck up here, and I'm afraid we can't get out to help you with the war.[69]

Besides the unknowns posed by the terrain, coalition planners wondered whether they might be falling into some kind of trap. It seemed incredible that the Iraqis would leave their flanks so unguarded. Military analysts say that one reason for Iraqi complacency may have been that they assumed that in addition to the rough terrain, the fine desert sand would cause too many mechanical problems for the armored vehicles. Such an assumption proved to be unfounded, since coalition tanks were far less prone to breakdowns than Iraqi tanks.

In any case, the flanking maneuver fit perfectly with Schwartzkopf's objective of using mobility, speed, and deception to surprise and then crush Saddam's Republican Guard divisions. Schwartzkopf was well aware that such speed and surprise were crucial if the coalition were to overcome its daunting forty-two-to-twelve disadvantage in divisions on the ground.

A Close Call

Yet on the eve of the ground war, the coalition came frighteningly close to losing its element of surprise. Iraq's foreign minister, Tariq Aziz, had recently visited Moscow. In an effort to convince the Iraqis that their situation was hopeless and that they should leave Kuwait, Soviet military experts showed Aziz updated satellite pictures taken only hours before. The photographs clearly showed the huge coalition force poised to cross the border west of Kuwait. Back in Baghdad, a shaken Aziz took the photographs to Saddam. But Saddam simply ignored the warning,

The Chemical Weapons Mystery

One of the great fears of the coalition as they went into battle was that the Iraqis would use chemical weapons. In his book *Desert Victory*, Norman Friedman pondered why they never did:

> Perhaps the greatest surprise was that the Iraqis never used gas. There was no question that they had it, and many U.S. officers expected it. On the other hand, they had been heavily leafletted with threats of dire consequences if gas were used. It may be also that, despite Saddam Hussein's public statement that his corps commanders could use gas whenever they wanted to, they still had to wait for specific orders from Baghdad. The word could not come over jammed and destroyed channels. It is also possible that individual Iraqi unit commanders were leery of using gas for fear that their own troops would die if the gas clouds drifted the wrong way or if gas shells burst as they were being loaded (both quite common risks). It turned out that the Iraqis' gas masks were largely worn out (as was first suspected from the condition of masks carried by deserters encountered early in the war).

believing instead that it was a Soviet deception made in concert with the Americans. Still convinced that the attack would come through eastern Kuwait, he made no moves to counter an attack from the west.

According to defense analyst Jeffrey Record, this episode illustrates just how destructive Saddam's terrorizing of his inner circle had been. "It forms as yet one more proof of Saddam's paranoia when confronted with unpleasant realities," wrote Record. "The apparent unwillingness of Tariq Aziz to insist that his boss face reality is further testimony to the utter servility and fear that pervaded Iraq's decision-making process."[70]

Rumbling into Iraq

On the afternoon of February 24, nine thousand wheeled vehicles of the 1st Armored Division and then the 3rd Armored Division rolled across the unguarded Iraqi border. They were the heart of the VII Corps, which had been given the mission of finding, attacking, and destroying the top four divisions of Saddam's elite Republican Guard divisions. Under Franks, the VII Corps had been built up into a huge attack force. Franks had 142,000 soldiers under his command, as well as more than 48,000 vehicles, including 1,500 tanks and 223 attack helicopters.

Once they crossed into Iraq, the two armored divisions would be on the move both day and night. Navigation in the desert is notoriously difficult, particularly at night. But recently developed technology made this previously impossible feat possible. Global positioning systems allowed units to know exactly where they were no matter how dark it was. Furthermore, as noted in *The Whirlwind War*, the official history of the U.S. Army's involvement in Iraq, an innovation by Henry Croley of the Army Materiel Command proved invaluable:

> Command and control, as well as protection against fratricide, were accomplished with the transmitting device Budd Light, named for its inventor, Henry C. "Budd" Croley of the Army Materiel Command. Consisting of infrared light-emitting diodes snapped onto the tops of commercial batteries, Budd Lights were placed on vehicle antennas in varying numbers to distinguish command or guide vehicles from others. Easily visible up to 1.2 miles through night vision goggles, the pur-plish glow of 10,000 Budd Lights enabled the 24th Division and other units to move safely at night.[71]

Enemy Ahead

After climbing out onto flatter terrain north of the border, the coalition attack force made a sharp turn to the right and roared eastward across the desert toward their Iraqi counterparts. They were arrayed in triangular wedges some fifteen miles wide. Around 7:00 P.M. on February 26, intelligence confirmed that a brigade of the Tawakalna Armored Division, with at least one hundred armored vehicles, was dug in a few miles away.

This first encounter with the Republican Guard would indicate just how dangerous Saddam's best divisions were. Their most formidable weapon was the Soviet-made T-72 tank with its giant 125 mm main gun. In assessing the strength of the Iraqi armored divisions, Carhart noted that "their star tank, the Soviet T-72, had long been trumpeted by Soviet salesmen as being the equal of, or even superior to, the U.S. M1A1 Abrams tank."[72]

In preparation for battle, the 1st Division tanks broke out of their wedges and came up together in one continuous line. Just to their south, the 3rd Division did the same. Sandstorms and smoke from burning oil fields made it hard to see even twenty feet with the naked eye, but now the Americans' superior night-vision and thermal-imaging devices allowed them to coordinate their movements in spite of the darkness. Sergeant First Class Anthony Steede, commander of one of the sixty-three-ton M1A1 tanks, later recalled the awesome sight of tanks from horizon to horizon as seen through his night-vision goggles.

As the battalion rumbled forward, each gunner kept his eyes glued on the thermal sights, looking for hot spots indicating Iraqi tanks or armor. Before long, Steede's gunner locked his laser-guided sights on a T-72 tank traversing a ridge nearly two miles off. Although he had never fired at a target that distant, the gunner requested permission to shoot. Meanwhile, Steede was waiting for the word to fire to come from his company commander. When it came, he hesitated a split second, then yelled, "Send it!"[73]

Flashbulbs and Bowling Balls

The tank-penetrating projectile used by Abrams tanks is called a sabot. It is an extremely dense metal rod with fins like the feathers on an arrow. A sabot round travels at about eighty-four hundred miles per hour. Upon piercing an enemy tank it tends to ignite everything inside. When

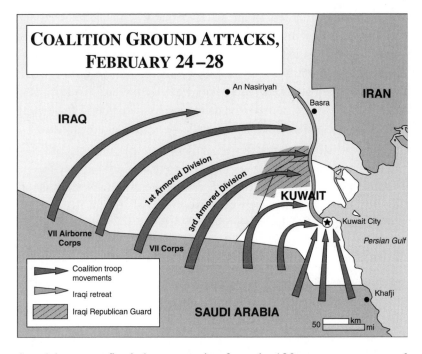

COALITION GROUND ATTACKS, FEBRUARY 24–28

IRAN

An Nasiriyah

Basra

IRAQ

1st Armored Division

3rd Armored Division

KUWAIT

Kuwait City

VII Airborne Corps

VII Corps

Persian Gulf

Coalition troop movements

Iraqi retreat

Iraqi Republican Guard

SAUDI ARABIA

Khafji

50 | km
| mi

Steede's gunner fired, the concussion from the 120 mm cannon seemed to lift the tank's front end off the ground. Steede closed his eyes to preserve his night vision, opening them just in time to pick up the tiny white dot on the end of the sabot round before it hit.

Then there was a sharp, white explosion—like a flashbulb popping. As Steede watched through his thermal sights, he saw jets of flame shoot out of the two hatches on top of the tank. A few seconds later, the onboard ammunition cooked off, sending the tank's ten-ton turret flying skyward.

Steede's spectacular kill was quickly followed by many more. Up and down the line, tanks fired at targets a mile or two ahead. As the sabot rounds hit, explosion after explosion rocked the horizon. A hail of gunfire greeted the coalition as they approached enemy positions, but Iraqi machine guns had no effect on the heavy tanks, and the T-72s were firing with little accuracy. Within seconds after giving away its position by firing a round, a T-72 would take a sabot round and be destroyed in a blinding flash.

As the advancing U.S. forces peered through their thermal sights, they were puzzled by green spots the size of bowling balls apparently suspended some ten feet in the air. Eventually someone realized that what they were seeing were the heads of Iraqi tank commanders who were standing inside tanks whose engines had been shut off to avoid detection. The Iraqis were cranking their turrets around by hand in hopes of targeting their attackers before they were seen. Word passed quickly that the green spots needed to be dealt with immediately. The bowling balls soon disappeared as the Iraqi tanks beneath them exploded.

No Time to Rest

In two hours of fighting, fifty-six T-72s and nearly a hundred Iraqi armored personnel carriers were destroyed. The 1st and 3rd Armored divisions had crushed a brigade of Saddam's best troops without losing a

Swollen Ankles and Soaked Soldiers

Ironically, much of the ground war in the Iraqi desert was fought under unusually rainy conditions. As members of the 1st Armored Division raced toward their ambush of Saddam's Republican Guard, they had to forgo sleep. And, as explained in *Triumph Without Victory,* a book compiled by the staff of *U.S. News & World Report,* conditions inside the tanks were far from comfortable:

> They were wet, cold, and tired. They had been driving in their cramped tank quarters for more than three days. The M1A1 Abrams tank was heated to ward off the cold of the desert night, and its ride was well cushioned as it raced across the bumpy desert floor. But to see where they were going and watch for the enemy, the tank commander and his loader had to stand up and look out their turret hatches. They were quickly soaked by the pouring rain. The water had run down their faces and into their chemical-protection suits, filling their boots. "You're just saturated with water," said Sergeant Jeffrey Reamer, the commander of an M1A1 tank in the 1st Armored Division's 1-35 Armor Battalion. "And you still have to do your job. Every tank commander I know, their ankles swelled up because they had to stand in the rain for so long." Below in the turrret and just forward of the tank commander sat the gunner. He was protected from the elements. But because the tank commander and the loader insisted that the heat be turned up as high as possible to keep them warm, the gunners baked in the tanks' interiors. Up front, the driver sat all alone in a reclining seat in a hole hardly bigger than a race-car cockpit. Above him was a heavy round hatch. The seal around it leaked profusely, and the M1A1 drivers sat in the pools of water that collected on their plastic seats.

single American soldier. It was an incredibly one-sided victory, but there was no time to celebrate. After refueling and rearming, the 1st Armored Division pushed on.

By dawn the next morning, three brigades of Abrams and Bradley fighting vehicles were heading eastward shoulder to shoulder. Shortly before noon, units of Saddam's Medina Armored Division were detected about a mile and a half away. At that point, the 1st Division's front was made up solely of M1A1 tanks—some 350 of them. Permission to fire was given and the battle of Medina Ridge began.

Outdrawing the Iraqis

As before, the M1A1s' laser-guided firing systems proved far superior to those of the Iraqi tanks—even the T-72s. A key factor was that the Americans' thermal sights allowed them to "see" much farther in the dark than their Iraqi counterparts. Despite heavy camouflage, enemy targets were destroyed long before American tanks could be seen with the naked eye.

Once again, flaws in Iraqi training were apparent. Not only did the M1A1s have greater range, but in a confrontation their crews were much quicker on the draw. At one point, Sergeant First Class "Scag" Scaglione and his tank were stopped at the head of the 1-35 Armor Battalion, part of the 1st Armored Division. Scaglione's tank was standing guard while the tanks behind stopped for a moment to repostion their unfired rounds. Suddenly, a T-72 came up over a ridge and aimed at Scaglione's company commander's tank, several hundred yards away. Scaglione swung his turret around and laid the crosshairs on the Iraqi tank. His gunner fired instantly, knocking out the tank before its crew could fire. In the next few minutes, Scaglione's crew destroyed three other approaching T-72s before they could even get off a shot.

Griffith, the commander of the 1st Division, watched all this from a Humvee parked on high ground directly behind the Second Brigade. It was an unforgettable scene. Against a backdrop of black clouds from burning oil fields, countless burning Iraqi vehicles flickered bright orange. Every few seconds, another "flashbulb" went off, marking the destruction of another enemy tank or armored vehicle. Meanwhile, the rumble of artillery and tank guns mixed with the sounds of real thunder. Occasionally, lightning bolts snaked across the sky. Griffith leaned close to an aide and said, "Take a good, long, hard look, son. You'll never see anything like this again."[74]

A Triumph of Technology

The strategy of mounting a massive ambush on Saddam's top tank units was fully vindicated on February 26 and 27. The plan was spectacularly successful. In *Iron Soldiers*, Carhart noted that the division "had attacked and fought victoriously across the desert some 300 kilometers [180 miles] in 89 hours, a lightning-bolt invasion unsurpassed in military history."[75] During their sprint across the desert, the 1st Armored Division lost four M1A1 tanks, two Bradley M2A2 tanks, an ambulance, two Apache helicopters, a fuel truck, and two Humvees. In the same period of time they destroyed 440 Iraqi tanks, 485 armored personnel carriers, 190 artillery pieces, and 1,383 trucks.

As the lopsided totals indicate, coalition tanks were superior in every way. Their computerized, laser-guided guns proved extraordinarily accurate. Onboard ballistic computers instantly analyzed the proper firing

Columns of armored vehicles move to engage Iraqi forces. The superior weaponry of the coalition forces facilitated their victory in the conflict.

Iraqi soldiers lie dead before a destroyed T-72 tank in the wake of the coalition's ground campaign.

angle, adjusting for wind speed, humidity, and type of ammunition—even as the tanks rolled forward over rough ground. Their range was equally impressive: They hit and destroyed Iraqi tanks at distances up to and even greater than two miles. Meanwhile, because they could continue shooting while on the move, coalition tanks made elusive targets.

But even when they could not move, the M1A1s' armor made them nearly indestructible. One particularly revealing incident took place when an M1A1 from the 24th Infantry Division became stuck in the mud. The rest of the unit had gone ahead while the tank remained to wait for a recovery vehicle. Suddenly, three T-72s came over a ridge and attacked. The first fired from just over a half mile away, hitting the M1A1's front armor with a shaped-charge (high-explosive) round.

On February 28, 1991, President Bush announces the cease-fire ending the Persian Gulf War. The war lasted exactly one hundred hours.

The hit did no damage. Meanwhile, the M1A1 crew returned fire with a 120 mm round that pierced the T-72 and blew its turret into the air.

The second T-72 also scored a direct hit on the Abrams that did no damage. When it turned to run, the M1A1 put a 120 mm round into its engine compartment and blew the engine into the air. The third T-72 fired a round from only a quarter mile away that did nothing more than leave a groove in the M1A1's frontal armor. It then retreated behind a sand berm. The M1A1 crew then blew up the Iraqi tank with a sabot round that traveled through the berm before piercing the enemy tank.

Other star performers were the Apache tank-destroying helicopters and coalition artillery. Using computer-calculated firing angles, coalition artillery quickly silenced Iraqi artillery. Coalition artillery was so effective that after a while, the Iraqis were afraid to fire their guns. The combination of technological advances and the well-trained soldiers who used them was devastating to Saddam's armored forces. Of Saddam's more than four thousand tanks, it is estimated that only seven hundred survived the war.

The Hundred-Hour War

Combat itself lasted exactly one hundred hours. At 8:00 A.M. Iraqi time on February 28, Bush surprised the world with a brief television speech. At the time, the remnants of Saddam's Republican Guard were nearly encircled near the city of Basra. Instead of forcing them to disarm, Bush announced a cease-fire, declaring Kuwait liberated and the Iraqi army defeated. "Seven months ago, America and the world drew a line in the sand," said the president. "We declared that the aggression aginst Kuwait would not stand, and tonight America and the world have kept their word."[76]

A Military to Be Proud Of

Rick Atkinson's summing up of the Gulf War in *Crusade: The Untold Story of the Persian Gulf War* made note of the fact that the conflict had given the military a new sense of itself:

> For twenty years the debacle of Vietnam had bred self-reproach, mistrust, and abiding doubt in the efficacy of military power. The competence and potency of the American military were now beyond question.

> "It is not big armies that win battles," Maurice de Saxe noted in 1732. "It is the good ones." The United States had built a military that was both big *and* good. The nation demonstrated that superpower status was calculated not simply in nuclear megatonnage but also in more prosaic capabilities: only America could have amassed more than nine million tons of materiel, hauled it six thousand miles to the Middle East, fought a war, then carted the stuff home again. . . . All in all, weapons and tactics worked well, troops performed with admirable skill, commanders showed themselves equal to the challenge.

The scorched remains of civilian and military vehicles, destroyed during the war, line the highway from Kuwait City to Basra.

Defense analyst Michael Mazarr and his coauthors, Don Snider and James Blackwell Jr., summed up what had been accomplished in such an incredibly short time:

> For four straight days and nights (without sleep) . . . the coalition forces had battled the Iraqi army into submission while traveling hundreds of miles. They destroyed thousands of Iraqi tanks, armored personnel carriers, and artillery pieces in perhaps the most fast-paced blitzkrieg in history. Enemy prisoners of war were estimated at over 58,000 with estimates of Iraqi casualties varying widely between 25,000 and 10,000. The coalition, in contrast, lost fewer than 200 due to enemy action, and less than 2,000 were wounded. Only a handful of coalition tanks were lost in combat.[77]

Lieutenant General Tom Kelly made a similar point with one colorful statement. "Iraq," he said, "went from the fourth-largest army in the world to the second-largest army in Iraq in 100 hours."[78]

Saddam No Strategist

Lieutenant Colonel Keith Alexander, the intelligence officer for the 1st Armored Division, was impressed by the Iraqi defenses, if not by their professionalism. He believed that had they fought hard, they could have probably taken out 10 percent of his division. Fortunately, most elected to surrender instead. "We got to practice on a third-stringer," said Alexander. "We were the New York Giants scrimmaging the JayVees [junior varsity] from some high school called the Iraqi 26th Division."[79]

In view of the less-than-impressive Iraqi performance during the war, Schwartzkopf was invited to give his personal assessment of Saddam's abilities as a military strategist. He made little effort to hide his true feelings. "Ha! As far as Saddam Hussein being a great military strategist, he is neither a strategist, nor is he schooled in the operational arts, nor is he a tactician, nor is he a general, nor is he a soldier," Schwartzkopf snorted. "Other than that, he's a great military man."[80]

In *Desert Storm*, the authors suggest that when it came to military matters, Saddam did more than anyone to ensure his own defeat:

> In the Gulf War it often seemed that Saddam Hussein was planning and executing his strategy to put U.S. precision weapons on display. He began a conflict in a largely flat and featureless

terrain easily scanned for activity by U.S. satellites and aircraft, at a time of year when the United States would be able
to wage warfare unencumbered by bad weather. Once he had
created this target-rich and smart bomb–friendly environment,
Saddam sat back, waited for us to initiate war and cripple his
air defenses, and then allowed us to conduct a devastating
month-long air campaign from the invulnerable sanctuary of
Saudi Arabia and other surrounding nations. Finally, he did
not feed or supply his troops adequately; his arbitrary and brutal decisions (beginning with the choice to invade Kuwait in
the first place) undercut his commands and demoralized his
troops—they had very little to fight for.[81]

An Unsatisfying

Epilogue Aftermath

A LTHOUGH SADDAM WAS humiliated by his forced withdrawal from Kuwait and Iraq's stinging military defeat, he managed to retain enough of his military arsenal to remain in power. In the months following the withdrawal from Kuwait, he used the surviving units of the Republican Guard to put down insurrections in Iraq's north and south with characteristic brutality.

Saddam's survival and the consolidation of his power was not the outcome Bush had in mind when he declared a cease-fire. Some in his administration had hoped the defeat would embolden the Iraqi people to rise up against Saddam and perhaps unite with the remnants of the army to form a more enlightened regime. Instead, Saddam was able to continue his reign of terror against anyone who opposed him.

The cease-fire had been announced because Bush believed all the coalition objectives had been achieved—Saddam had been evicted from Kuwait and his army had been severely punished. While the coalition could easily have pushed on to Baghdad, that would have almost certainly have meant many more casualties on both sides.

The Wrong Message?

In his book *Hollow Victory*, defense analyst Jeffrey Record noted how the cease-fire may have sent an unintended message to Saddam:

> Rarely in history has a victorious army unilaterally stopped fighting —*in the absence of any request for terms by the vanquished*; and a man with Saddam Hussein's mentality almost certainly interpreted Bush's haste in unilaterally calling off the

Iraqi soldiers surrender to U.S. forces the day before the cease-fire is declared. Although the cease-fire brought an end to the conflict, Saddam remained in power.

war as a sign of weakness. Indeed, in a speech "celebrating" the first anniversary of Desert Storm's beginning, Saddam pointedly remarked: "It was George Bush with his own will who decided to stop the fighting. Nobody had asked him to do so."[82]

The behavior of members of Saddam's Republican Guard also suggested that they viewed the cease-fire as a sign of weakness. That was the prevailing impression by the tank crews of Colonel Montgomery Meigs's brigade of the 1st Armored Division. Near Basra they had to stand by idly while surviving members of the Republican Guard taunted them. "We could see them out there at 600 and 700 meters [2,000–2,300 feet], waving at us, waving their weapons, and just walking away," recalled Sergeant Anthony Widner. "These were the guys who had been shooting at us earlier."[83] The Iraqis' defiant attitude convinced Widner and many others that the fighting had stopped a little too soon.

Schwartzkopf agreed. In a television interview after the cease-fire he expressed his own frustration:

> Frankly, my recommendation had been, you know, to continue the march. I mean, we had them in a rout and could have continued to wreak great destruction on them. We could have completely closed the doors and made it in fact a battle of annihilation. . . . There were obviously a lot of people who escaped who wouldn't have escaped if the decision hadn't been made to stop where we were at the time.[84]

Business as Usual

There is little question that the timing of the cease-fire was beneficial to Saddam. Record's opinion is shared by many. "It is certainly clear in retrospect," he noted, "that the cease-fire's timing permitted significant Iraqi forces to escape to fight another day."[85] An estimated 700 tanks, 1,430 armored personnel carriers, and 110,000 troops were allowed to leave the battle zone. Saddam had need of them almost immediately.

"Suckering" Schwartzkopf

In *Victory Without Triumph*, reporters from *U.S. News & World Report* noted how Saddam found a way to slaughter the Kurds and still remain within the terms of the cease-fire:

> The terms of the cease-fire had also allowed the Iraqi army to fly helicopters. General Schwartzkopf insisted that the Iraqis fly no fixed-wing aircraft, but he assented to the use of the helicopters when the Iraqi generals said they needed them to transport wounded soldiers and for other tasks. Schwartzkopf said days afterward that he was "suckered" by the Iraqis. By then, Saddam Hussein's soldiers were firing from the helicopters at the hapless Kurds in the mountains of northern Iraq. It is certain that Saddam's Republican Guard would have quelled the Kurdish uprising ultimately. But in the difficult terrain of the mountains, the helicopters turned what might have been a negotiated truce into a massacre. While the Bush administration sent aid to the Kurdish refugees (after an embarassing international outcry), it never raised a finger to prevent the slaughter by soldiers in helicopters.

Within hours of the cease-fire talks, Shiite Muslims in southern Iraq rose up against Saddam's rule. In the northern part of the country, the ethnic group known as the Kurds also rebelled.

Moving first to put down the Shiite rebellion, Saddam's men fared much better against nearly defenseless civilians than they had against an opposing army. His Republican Guard strafed crowds of civilians, poured gasoline on the wounded and set them afire, and publicly hung captives as examples. Once the southern uprising had been stifled, Saddam turned his full attention to the Kurds.

Thousands were massacred, some with poison gas. Others were killed with tanks, artillery, and rocket-firing helicopter gunships. When the carnage ended, thousands were dead and Saddam was still firmly in control of the country. Meanwhile, economic sanctions placed on Iraq caused great hardship on ordinary Iraqis—but not on Saddam—for the next decade.

The end result of Saddam's aggression was eerily similar to the situation after the Iran-Iraq War. Billions of dollars of military hardware had been destroyed and the country weakened and impoverished. Thousands of Iraqis were dead or wounded for little purpose. But the bottom line for Saddam was that he was still in power—which, many analysts contend, had been his ultimate motivation for launching the invasion of Kuwait in the first place.

Notes

Introduction: The Seizure of Kuwait

1. Quoted in Jeffrey Record, *Hollow Victory: A Contrary View of the Gulf War.* New York: Brassey's, 1993, p. 30.
2. Quoted in Judith Miller and Laurie Mylroie, *Saddam Hussein and the Crisis in the Gulf.* New York: Times Books, 1990, p. 215.
3. Quoted in Elaine Sciolino, *The Outlaw State: Saddam Hussein's Quest for Power and the Gulf Crisis.* New York: Wiley, 1991, p. 207.
4. Quoted in Miller and Mylroie, *Saddam Hussein and the Crisis in the Gulf*, p. 212.
5. Quoted in Miller and Mylroie, *Saddam Hussein and the Crisis in the Gulf*, p. 213.
6. Quoted in Sciolino, *Outlaw State*, p. 224.
7. Quoted in Sciolino, *Outlaw State*, p. 205.

Chapter 1: Dreaming of Nebuchadnezzar

8. Quoted in Sciolino, *Outlaw State*, p. 61.
9. Norman Friedman, *Desert Victory: The War for Kuwait.* Annapolis, MD: Naval Institute Press, 1991, pp. 16–17.
10. Quoted in Sciolino, *Outlaw State*, p. 63.
11. Quoted in R. Watson and R. Wilkinson, "Baghdad's Bully," *Newsweek*, August 13, 1990.
12. Quoted in O. Friedrich and Dan Goodgame, "Master of His Universe," *Time*, August 13, 1990.
13. Friedrich and Goodgame, "Master of his Universe."
14. Quoted in Sciolino, *Outlaw State*, p. 50.
15. Quoted in Sciolino, *Outlaw State*, p. 50.
16. Quoted in Miller and Mylroie, *Saddam Hussein and the Crisis in the Gulf*, p. 57.
17. Quoted in Efraim Karsh and Inari Rautsi, *Saddam Hussein: A Political Biography.* New York: Free Press, 1991, p. 124.

18. Miller and Mylroie, *Saddam Hussein and the Crisis in the Gulf,* p. 54.
19. Quoted in Karsh and Rautsi, *Saddam Hussein,* p.206.
20. Quoted in Sciolino, *Outlaw State,* p. 77.
21. Quoted in Miller and Mylroie, *Saddam Hussein and the Crisis in the Gulf,* p. 41.
22. Quoted in Record, *Hollow Victory,* p. 20.

Chapter 2: Saddam Against the World

23. Record, *Hollow Victory,* p. 74.
24. Quoted in Turi Munthe, ed., *The Saddam Hussein Reader: Selections from Leading Writers on Iraq.* New York: Thunder's Mouth Press, 2002, p. 269.
25. Quoted in *U.S. News & World Report, Triumph Without Victory: The Unreported History of the Persian Gulf War.* New York: Times Books, 1993, p. 95.
26. Quoted in Michael J. Mazarr, Don M. Snider, and James A. Blackwell Jr., *Desert Storm: The Gulf War and What We Learned.* Boulder, CO: Westview Press, 1993, p. 46.
27. Quoted in Sciolino, *Outlaw State,* p. 182.
28. Quoted in Record, *Hollow Victory,* p. 47.
29. Friedman, *Desert Victory,* p. 69.
30. Quoted in Sciolino, *Outlaw State,* p. 236.
31. Quoted in Mazarr, Snider, and Blackwell, *Desert Storm,* p. 67.
32. Quoted in Mazarr, Snider, and Blackwell, *Desert Storm,* p. 67.
33. Quoted in *U.S. News & World Report, Triumph Without Victory,* pp. 195–96.
34. Quoted in Sciolino, *Outlaw State,* p. 242.
35. Quoted in Mazarr, Snider, and Blackwell, *Desert Storm,* p. 84.
36. Quoted in *U.S. News & World Report, Triumph Without Victory,* pp. 205–206.
37. Raphael Patai, *The Arab Mind,* rev. ed. New York: Hatherleigh Press, 2002, pp. 228–29.
38. Record, *Hollow Victory,* p. 38.
39. Quoted in Mazarr, Snider, and Blackwell, *Desert Storm,* p. 80.
40. Quoted in Mazarr, Snider, and Blackwell, *Desert Storm,* pp. 90–91.
41. Quoted in Mazarr, Snider, and Blackwell, *Desert Storm,* p. 91.

Chapter 3: No Shelter from the Storm

42. Quoted in Friedman, *Desert Victory,* p. 93.
43. Rick Atkinson, *Crusade: The Untold Story of the Persian Gulf War.*

Boston: Houghton Mifflin, 1993, p. 36.

44. Quoted in *U.S. News & World Report, Triumph Without Victory*, p. 218.

45. Mazarr, Snider, and Blackwell, *Desert Storm*, p. 97.

46. *U.S. News & World Report, Triumph Without Victory*, p. 228.

47. Atkinson, *Crusade*, p. 37.

48. Quoted in *U.S. News & World Report, Triumph Without Victory*, p. 224.

49. James F. Dunnigan and Austin Bay, *From Shield to Storm: High-Tech Weapons, Military Strategy, and Coalition Warfare in the Persian Gulf.* New York: William Morrow, 1992, p. 156.

50. Mazarr, Snider, and Blackwell, *Desert Storm*, p. 108.

51. Friedman, *Desert Victory*, p. 162.

52. Quoted in Atkinson, *Crusade*, p. 82.

53. Mazarr, Snider, and Blackwell, *Desert Storm*, p. 107.

54. Sciolino, *Outlaw State*, p. 255.

Chapter 4: The Mother of All Retreats

55. Quoted in *U.S. News & World Report, Triumph Without Victory*, p. 271.

56. Friedman, *Desert Victory*, p. 162.

57. Atkinson, *Crusade*, p. 212.

58. Quoted in Mazarr, Snider, and Blackwell, *Desert Storm*, pp. 131–32.

59. Quoted in Sciolino, *Outlaw State*, p. 257.

60. Dunnigan and Bay, *From Shield to Storm*, p. 267.

61. Quoted in Sciolino, *Outlaw State*, p. 259.

62. Quoted in *U.S. News & World Report, Triumph Without Victory*, p. 296.

63. Molly Moore, *A Woman at War: Storming Kuwait with the U.S. Marines.* New York: Scribner's, 1993, p. 204.

64. Quoted in *U.S. News & World Report, Triumph Without Victory*, p. 324.

65. Mazarr, Snider, and Blackwell, *Desert Victory*, p. 149.

Chapter 5: Ambush in the Desert

66. Tom Carhart, *Iron Soldiers*. New York: Pocket Books, 1994, p. 54.

67. Carhart, "Iron Soldiers, p. 124.

68. Quoted in Carhart, *Iron Soldiers*, pp. 127–28.

69. Quoted in Carhart, *Iron Soldiers*, p. 126.

70. Record, *Hollow Victory*, p. 90.

71. Frank N. Schubert and Theresa L. Kraus, eds., *The Whirlwind War:*

The United States Army in Operations Desert Shield and Desert Storm, U.S. Army Center of Military History pub. no. 70–30. Washington, DC: U.S. Government Printing Office, 1995, p. 177.

72. Carhart, *Iron Soldiers*, p. 55.
73. Quoted in Carhart, *Iron Soldiers*, p. 31.
74. Quoted in Carhart, *Iron Soldiers*, pp. 296–97.
75. Carhart, *Iron Soldiers*, p. 324.
76. Quoted in Sciolino, *Outlaw State*, p. 261.
77. Mazarr, Snider, and Blackwell, *Desert Victory*, pp. 156–57.
78. Quoted in Michael Martin, "Desert Ambush," *Heartland USA*, September/October 2002, p. 35.
79. Quoted in *U.S. News & World Report, Triumph Without Victory*, p. 321.
80. Quoted in Sciolino, *Outlaw State*, p. 261.
81. Mazarr, Snider, and Blackwell, *Desert Storm*, p. 113.

Epilogue: An Unsatisfying Aftermath

82. Record, *Hollow Victory*, p. 126.
83. Quoted in *U.S. News & World Report, Triumph Without Victory*, p. 400.
84. Quoted in Record, *Hollow Victory*, p. 125.
85. Record, *Hollow Victory*, p. 125.

Chronology

August 2, 1990
Iraq invades Kuwait.

August 5
President George H.W. Bush declares that the invasion "will not stand."

August 6
Saudi Arabia asks for U.S. military assistance.

August 8
The first U.S. fighter planes begin arriving in Saudi Arabia.

November 8
Bush announces a doubling of U.S. forces in Saudi Arabia.

November 29
The UN Security Council authorizes use of force to remove Iraq from Kuwait.

January 9, 1991
Secretary of State James Baker meets with Iraqi representatives in Geneva, Switzerland, in an unsuccessful effort to find a peaceful solution.

January 12
U.S. Congress authorizes use of force to evict Iraqis from Kuwait.

January 15
UN deadline for Iraqi withdrawal from Kuwait passes.

January 17
Coalition attack begins in early morning hours.

January 18
First Scud missiles hit Israel.

January 29

Iraqis mount an attack against Saudi town of Khafji.

February 24

After five weeks of bombing, coalition forces begin ground attack.

February 25

Due to unexpected successes, VII Corps begins move into Iraq a day early.

February 26

As coalition forces approach Kuwait City, Saddam announces a withdrawal and Iraqi forces flee. North of Kuwait, VII Corps begins destroying elements of Saddam's Republican Guard.

February 27

The 24th Infantry Division attacks toward Basra while the 1st Armored Division decimates the Medina Division of the Republican Guard. Kuwait City is liberated and Bush and his advisers agree to stop the war.

February 28

Cease-fire takes effect at 8 A.M.

For Further Reading

Books

Dale Anderson, *Saddam Hussein*. Minneapolis, MN: Lerner, 2004. This biography of the Iraqi dictator covers his life up through the second Gulf War.

Fred Bratman, *War in the Persian Gulf*. Brookfield, CT: Millbrook Press, 1991. A concise history of the war, with particular emphasis on the importance of oil in its genesis.

Paul J. Deegan, *Operation Desert Storm*. Edina, MN: Abdo and Daughters, 1991. An account of the military campaigns that ended Iraq's occupation of Kuwait.

Kathlyn Gay and Martin Gay, *Persian Gulf War*. New York: Twenty-First Century Books, 1996. Focuses more on the events that led to the war than on the war itself, but provides excellent background on why Iraq felt Kuwait was fair game for an invasion.

Tracey Reavis, *Stealth Jet Fighter: The F-117A*. New York: Childrens Press, 2000. Discusses the development and history of the aerial star of Operation Desert Storm, as well as some of the missions it flew during the war.

Internet Sources

Frontline, "The Gulf War: An In-Depth Examination of the 1990–1991 Persian Gulf Crisis," 1996. www.pbs.org/wgbh/pages/frontline/gulf. An excellent site that examines the war through the words of military and political leaders as well as the soldiers who fought it. Plenty of audio links add to its value.

In Depth Info, "The Gulf War," 2004. www.indepthinfo.com/iraq/
index.shtml. Provides a good capsule history of the conflict.

Washington Post, "Fog of War: The 1991 Air Battle for Baghdad," 1998.
www.washingtonpost.com/wp-srv/inatl/longterm/fogofwar/
fogofwar.htm. This *Washington Post* Web site chronicles the air
war over Baghdad in great detail and includes many photographs
of the resulting bomb damage.

Works Consulted

Books

Rick Atkinson, *Crusade: The Untold Story of the Persian Gulf War.* Boston: Houghton Mifflin, 1993. A thorough and balanced account of the war by a Pulitzer Prize–winning reporter who conducted more than five hundred interviews to get as many different perspectives as possible.

Phyllis Bennis and Michel Moushabeck, eds., *Beyond the Storm: A Gulf Crisis Reader.* Brooklyn, NY: Olive Branch Press, 1991. A collection of thirty-one essays about Saddam and the situation he created by the invasion of Kuwait.

Tom Carhart, *Iron Soldiers.* New York: Pocket Books, 1994. Details the exploits of the 1st Armored Division as they swept into Iraq to deliver a "left hook" to Saddam's best troops. The battles, often told from the perspective of the men who fought them, make for riveting reading. Clearly illustrates the awesome might of the M1A1 tank.

Andrew Cockburn and Patrick Cockburn, *Out of the Ashes: The Resurrection of Saddam Hussein.* New York: HarperCollins, 1999. An analysis of what happened in Iraq after the Gulf War, including vivid accounts of the brutality Saddam used to ensure he remained in power.

James F. Dunnigan and Austin Bay, *From Shield to Storm: High-Tech Weapons, Military Strategy, and Coalition Warfare in the Persian Gulf.* New York: William Morrow, 1992. Two military historians recount the war with emphasis on the weapons that won it.

Norman Friedman, *Desert Victory: The War for Kuwait.* Annapolis, MD: Naval Institute Press, 1991. Puts the war in political and strategic context while providing a detailed analysis of what worked and what did not work militarily.

Hans Halberstadt, *Desert Storm Ground War.* Osceola, WI: Motorbooks International, 1991. A bare-bones account of the ground war accompanied by plenty of pictures.

Dilip Hiro, *The Longest War: The Iran-Iraq Military Conflict.* New York: Routledge, 1991. An account of the war Iraq fought before the Gulf War. Gives some insight into the techniques Saddam thought would work in the Gulf War.

Efraim Karsh and Inari Rautsi, *Saddam Hussein: A Political Biography.* New York: Free Press, 1991. A detailed and objective look at how Saddam Hussein rose to power and how his ambition led him into two catastrophic wars.

Michael Kelly, *Martyr's Day: Chronicle of a Small War.* New York: Random House, 1993. Personal observations of a *New York Times* reporter who poked around the Middle East before, during, and after the war.

Michael J. Mazarr, Don M. Snider, and James A. Blackwell Jr., *Desert Storm: The Gulf War and What We Learned.* Boulder, CO: Westview Press, 1993. A relatively short but balanced look at the military and foreign policy implications of the war.

Judith Miller and Laurie Mylroie, *Saddam Hussein and the Crisis in the Gulf.* New York: Times Books, 1990. Provides good background on Saddam's rise to power and his brutal methods of operation.

Molly Moore, *A Woman at War: Storming Kuwait with the U.S. Marines.* New York: Scribner's, 1993. The author, a reporter for the *Washington Post*, accompanied a marine general into battle and got a rare look at how the war was experienced by one of its leaders.

Turi Munthe, ed., *The Saddam Hussein Reader: Selections from Leading Writers on Iraq.* New York: Thunder's Mouth Press, 2002. Essays on Iraq from many different perspectives. Those on how Saddam came to power are particularly revealing of his brutal methods of operation.

Raphael Patai, *The Arab Mind*, rev. ed. New York: Hatherleigh Press, 2002. A classic book about the psychology of Arabs. Provides insight into why Saddam appears so irrational to Western minds.

John Pimlott and Stephen Badsey, and members of the Department of War Studies, Royal Military Academy, *The Gulf War Assessed.* London: Arms and Armour, 1992. An analysis of the war from the British perspective.

Jadranka Porter, *Under Siege in Kuwait: A Survivor's Story.* London: Victor Gollancz, 1991. The author was caught inside Kuwait City when Iraqi forces invaded. She explains what it was like to live in fear of being discovered and shot as a spy.

Jeffrey Record, *Hollow Victory: A Contrary View of the Gulf War.* New York: Brassey's, 1993.

Paul William Roberts, *The Demonic Comedy: Some Detours in the Baghdad of Saddam Hussein.* New York: Farrar, Straus and Giroux, 1998.

Frank N. Schubert and Theresa L. Kraus, eds. *The Whirlwind War: The United States Army in Operations Desert Shield and Desert Storm,* U.S. Army Center of Military History pub. no. 70–30. Washington, DC: U.S. Government Printing Office, 1995. A highly technical account of the army's role in the war.

Elaine Sciolino, *The Outlaw State: Saddam Hussein's Quest for Power and the Gulf Crisis.* New York: Wiley, 1991. A well-written account of Saddam's rise to power. More accessible than many such books since it does not go into great detail on the weapons used.

Geoff Simons, *Iraq: From Sumer to Saddam.* New York: St. Martin's Press, 1994. A broad history of Iraq, but the final chapter gives a detailed account of Saddam's actions during the war.

Jean Edward Smith, *George Bush's War.* New York: Henry Holt, 1992. Highly critical of the way the Persian Gulf War seemed to become a personal battle between Bush and Saddam.

Martin Stanton, *Road to Baghdad.* New York: Ballantine, 2003. The author, an American military adviser, was in Kuwait City on vacation when Saddam invaded and was later taken to Iraq and held as a hostage. A well-written and highly personal account. Sections on the immediate aftermath of the invasion underscore the lack of professionalism among Iraqi soldiers.

U.S. News & World Report, Triumph Without Victory: The Unreported History of the Persian Gulf War. New York: Times Books, 1993. A well-researched book that provides many behind-the-scenes looks at how U.S. military and political leaders wrestled with the problem of Saddam—and with each other.

Periodicals

O. Friedrich and Dan Goodgame, "Master of His Universe," *Time,* August 13, 1990.

Michael Martin, "Desert Ambush," *Heartland USA,* September/October 2002.

R. Watson and R. Wilkinson, "Baghdad's Bully," *Newsweek,* August 13, 1990.

Index

Picture Credits

About the Author

A former editor at *Reminisce* magazine, Michael J. Martin is a freelance writer whose home overlooks the Mississippi River in Lansing, Iowa. He has written more than a dozen books for young people, and his articles have appeared in magazines such as *Boys' Life*, *Timeline*, and *American History*. His most recent book for Lucent was *The Korean War: Life as a POW.*